C H

THE
CHICKEN
QABALAH

OF

RABBI LAMED BEN CLIFFORD

A Dilettante's Guide to
What You Do and *Do Not* Need to Know
to Become a Qabalist

LON MILO DUQUETTE

WEISER BOOKS
York Beach, Maine, USA

First published in 2001 by
WEISER BOOKS
P. O. Box 612
York Beach, ME 03910-0612
www.weiserbooks.com

Library of Congress Cataloging-in-Publication Data

DuQuette, Lon Milo.
    Chicken Qabalah of Rabbi Lamed Ben Clifford / Lon Milo
DuQuette.
        p. cm.
    Includes bibliographical references and index.
    ISBN 1-57863-215-3 (pbk.)
    1. Cabala. 2. Tarot. 3. Tree of life. 4. Gematria. 5. Cabala—Humor.
I. Title.

BF1611 .D869 2001
135'.47—dc21   2001017612

Typeset in 11/14 Adobe Garamond
Text design by Kathryn Sky-Peck
Back cover photo by Paul Martens

Printed in the United States of America

VG

08   07   06   05   04   03   02   01
     8   7   6   5   4   3   2   1

A
NEW
IMPROVED
QABALISTIC TEXT
OF GREAT CYNICISM AND WISDOM WRITTEN
EXPRESSLY FOR DILETTANTES WITH
REALLY SHORT ATTENTION SPANS
WHO PRETENTIOUSLY CONSIDER
THEMSELVES HERMETIC QABALISTS
BUT WHO ARE NONETHELESS SERIOUS
ABOUT UTILIZING A TINY PORTION OF THE
HEBREW QABALAH
FOR SPIRITUAL
ENLIGHTEN-
MENT.

ACKNOWLEDGMENTS

The author wishes to thank the following individuals who contributed to the manifestation of this work in the world of Assiah:

Constance Jean DuQuette, whose love and sense of humor has almost overcome her detestation of the Qabalah;

Rodney Orpheus, who interrupted his decadent life as rock star, recording artist, and globe-hopper to pen the Foreword;

Rabbi Gizmo Ben Lamed, who graciously opened his heart and his archives;

Ida Pengala, of *Augury Today*, and Dr. Terrence Stool of *Gomer* magazine;

Ms. Carolyn Tillie, who four years ago promised to reward me with a ten-course "Qabalistic" dinner if I were ever to write a book on the Qabalah.

CONTENTS

LIST OF FIGURES

MY LIFE WITH THE RABBI

By Rodney Orpheus

Let me begin by saying that no matter what Mr. DuQuette may be obliged to say in his introductory words, Rabbi Lamed Ben Clifford is (was) real. I, perhaps more than anyone else on Earth, understand the author's reasons for choosing to infer that the text represents a pseudepigraphic effort of his own. To men and women of integrity, a spiritual oath of secrecy is a serious and burdensome commitment, and Mr. DuQuette, by means of this elaborate literary charade, has obviously fulfilled his obligations admirably. I, on the other hand, am bound by no such covenants, and because I, too, am compiling a record of the events of my life with the Master, I am grateful to Mr. DuQuette for allowing me to share some of my memories.

It was a wet and stormy night when first I met the Rabbi Lamed Ben Clifford. I was a young chela of an occult Order then attending initiations in A....., a beautiful old German town. I remember the moment distinctly. I was standing on a stack of chairs wielding a huge Japanese katana, swinging it round with ease to impress the assembled neophytes with my skill in the oriental arts, when I was approached by a rotund figure, his beard wafting in the breeze from my blade.

"Little Brother!" he commanded me in a loud voice, "You have been meddling with the Qabalah!"

The throng around me seemed to shrink away at his imperious, if somewhat squeaky, voice. I stood transfixed by his gaze, the sword held high above my head. For a long second, there was no sound.

"No I haven't," I stated calmly, "But I don't mind having it meddle with me."

He looked at me quizzically, seeming to examine my face intently, then turned on his heel and walked away. In my mind I had a sudden flash of insight. I leapt down from my post and ran after him, throwing myself at his feet.

"Master!" I exclaimed, for I now knew I was in the presence of a member of that mystical, mythical Great White Brotherhood I had sought for so long, "Take me as your pupil—please!"

"I can't do that," he said, "The Qabalah is not for charismatic rock stars such as yourself. It can only be mastered by one who has already lived a full life. You must be married and have accumulated more wealth before you can study as a true Rabbi of the Lord."

"But Master, there must be a way—I'll be your secretary, clean your house, shine your shoes, anything! But I must learn the true knowledge behind the meaninglessness of Number and Symbol that is my only learning up until this moment."

"Well, pop by the house the next time you are in the States, we'll see what we have for you!" His eyes twinkled. I knew I'd been given a challenge. Did I have the dedication to throw away my life for this man, and become his servant in the Holy Wisdom of the Qabalah? Sure I did!

So it was, and months later I stepped off a plane in New York City, all my belongings packed in a small bag over my shoulder, in search of enlightenment. I had heard that the Rabbi ran a small community in Montauk, composed of only those true initiates that he had personally selected. However, try as I might, I knew of no one who knew the identity of even one of those initiates, so secretive was the Order to which they belonged. Over the next years I was to find out why.

The Order (I won't give its true name here) was descended from an ancient sect of Essenes who had begun the study of Qabalah after the fall of the biblical Tower of Babel. Their belief was, and is, that any who study the Holy Wisdom share the danger of those unwise

Master Builders of old, whose pride led Jehovah to punish them for daring to come before His Countenance. Thus the Order members vow themselves to complete anonymity on their initiation, so that the Lord cannot find and punish them for their spiritual hubris. Now I understood why the Rabbi, although versed in the wisdom of the Holy Qabalah like no man in this century, had published nothing; indeed his name was unknown even in the occult circles in which I had previously moved.

I was to become one of the lucky few intimates of the Rabbi during my stay. As his secretary, I had access to many of his communications— both material and spiritual. For the former, I was amazed at his contacts around the world. One would never know who he'd be talking to from one day to the next—from a bum in the street in Seattle ("one of the greatest magi currently alive," according to the Rabbi) to a leading politician in Europe ("well, he tries hard," spoken with a deep sigh).

His spiritual communications were no less intriguing—he spoke frequently to Goetic spirits and Enochian angels, often over afternoon tea (Earl Grey seemed especially efficacious for this purpose). I rapidly became proficient in shorthand, and always kept a pencil and pad handy—and an eraser, for, as the Rabbi put it: "Those guys can often benefit from a bit of judicious editing."

There were many sunny afternoons when we sat together in the garden over a huge pot of steaming tea while the Rabbi pontificated and argued with his Invisible Superiors over the future direction of the Order's work. The notes I took filled several boxes, and I was amazingly grateful for the invention of the Apple Macintosh computer which allowed me to finally dump the Rabbi's ancient Burroughs typing machine.

Always, always, I asked the Rabbi when I could become a full initiate of the Mysteries; and always received the same answer: that I must be more successful, more wealthy, married, and fruitful before I could even think of being considered as a potential Rabbi myself.

"But," I protested, "You need someone to carry on your work, Master!"

And in those moments his eyes would fall on the picture of Mr. DuQuette[1] that he kept on his desk, along with those of the other initiates.

"Perhaps . . . ," and he would say no more.

Be that as it may, I zealously continued my studies and practices, and eventually it became obvious to all at the Montauk center that I was becoming the Master's favorite. Naturally this gave rise to jealousy and the petty intrigues that are the bane of monastic societies.

My chief adversary was a quiet, passive-aggressive student who presumptuously renamed himself Gizmo Ben Lamed. He could type faster than I, and continually jockeyed for my position as Master's secretary. One day, in front of Master and the other pupils, he challenged me to a typing duel. Like a fool I accepted, for to decline would have meant instant victory for Ben Lamed.

My defeat was the beginning of the end for my career at Montauk. Gizmo continued to poison the minds of the members of the Order against me, and the Master advanced other neophytes while I was kept at a low degree. Still, I knew he secretly liked me more than the others, for as he was wont to quote on the many occasions when he cuffed me round the side of the head, "Whom I love, I chastise with many rods."

One day I could stand it no longer. I burst into the Master's sanctum. "I DEMAND to be finally made an initiate of the Qabalah!" I shouted, "Teach me the secrets that lie within the Numbers and the Cards!" Too late, the Rabbi was sitting hunched over his desk accompanied by Gizmo Ben Lamed, both intently examining what appeared to be an ancient Indian illustrated treatise on advanced magical techniques. They looked up at me.

"Impossible!" boomed the Master. "You are far too young and inexperienced. Why, you're not even married!" My face fell. He was right. He, on the other hand, had somehow tricked a beautiful young girl named Constance into his clutches years before. The rumor was that he had used certain forbidden magical methods to do so, but of that I have no proof—yet. But to continue my history . . .

Before I could answer, the Rabbi raised a restraining hand and turned to Gizmo. "He must be given a chance. He must do as our forefathers did, and go to the desert for 40 days and 40 nights to be tried in the pure sight of the Lord. If he survives, it will be clear proof that he has achieved the insignificance that befits a true member of our Order, and can be initiated in due course. Cuddles" (he always called Gizmo that name for reasons that are still unclear to me), "You will take him in the morning to be tried. He must find the limits of the City of God."

Gizmo glared at me, but even he could not go against the mighty Will of the Rabbi.

That night I could hardly sleep, no matter how comfortably I arranged my bed of gorse. In the morning I would finally get my chance to prove myself. I knew I could do it. Promptly about four hours after sunrise I heard the telltale sound of a Volkswagen camper pull up in the front yard. I ran out and jumped into the seat. Without a word I was blindfolded with a bright canary yellow cloth and we took off. We drove in silence for four days. I knew Ben Lamed and others in the van were burning with jealousy. How I would show them!

At high noon of the fourth day we stopped, and I was ceremoniously dumped out of the van, which roared off in an unknown direction. I took off my blindfold, took out my trusty Boy Scout knife, and began my walkabout through the desert, putting my faith in the Lord's ability to overlook me until I had found the sign I was looking for. For many days I walked, without real food and water (though I did find a McDonalds by the side of the road that helped a lot). I saw visions of angels with spreading dark wings and demons in the form of beautiful Thai women who tempted me with their slim seductive bodies. But still I prevailed, looking only for that sign that would show me the true Way that I desired.

Finally that day came. I had almost given up hope. My vision was blurred, my mind blank. I tottered on the brink of despair. Then I saw it. The sign. THE sign. The sign that I had looked for day and night since leaving New York:

Interstate

Las Vegas

City Limits

Here in a blinding flash was the answer I sought. For was it not man's True Will that raised us to the state between mere animal existence and divinity? And did not the Number 93 epitomize that True Will?[2] I had sought the limits of the City of God, and here they were, within my own Will, stated plainly within the Holy Qabalah. I marveled once again at the wisdom of Rabbi Lamed Ben Clifford who had brought me to this place, and at the materialization of the Qabalah upon Earth. Eagerly I strode forward to Las Vegas.

Once there I began my studies in earnest. I spent innumerable hours in the casinos, enmeshed in understanding the subtle patterns within the Numbers, the archetypal forces embodied in the Cards, and the Dionysian pleasures brought to me by the Lord's own cocktail waitresses. I knew that I could not return to the Rabbi without fulfilling the duties he had expounded to me, so for 40 days and nights I threw myself into my work with a passion.

My practical studies had led to great things. I was now a wealthy and successful man, with a lovely Asian wife I had found on the Internet. It was time to return to the bosom of the Rabbi. I packed my bags and set off for the Hermetic homeland of Montauk.

I turned up at the Rabbi's home. The days had not been kind to him. He looked old and worn, his arms held up by Gizmo Ben Lamed, who was unfortunately still around. I wasted no time in demanding to be finally initiated into the secrets of the Order. How could they refuse me now? I threw my bag down on my old familiar gorse and fell into a deep and satisfied sleep.

The morning dawned bright and clear, and I was brought before the Rabbi, now dressed as I had never before seen him, as a Priest of the Ancient Mysteries. For an old man, he still looked pretty good in a leopard skin. I cannot tell you details of the next seventeen hours, but at the end, he laid his hands upon me. His hands jerked convulsively upon my now-shaven head, pouring his magical essence into me, "I am now about to consecrate, ordain, raise, and confirm you, an initiate of the Mysteries of ....., now and forever. But first you will repeat after me the Terrible Oath of Secrecy."

He fell forward, his arms around me with joy. After a few minutes the position began to get a little uncomfortable, but I endured his weight nonetheless. I could hear Gizmo prompting the Rabbi with the Terrible Oath of Secrecy, but the Rabbi did not stir. Then his body slowly slid to the floor, a horrific expression on his face. He was dead.

The Doctor said it was pulmonary infarction. I knew better. With his initiation of me, his life's work was complete. I was now his Follower.

A few short months after this I received a call from my old friend, the famous occult editor (and fellow initiate) B., apprising me of Mr. DuQuette's intention to publish the Rabbi's legendary lost manuscripts on the *Chicken Qabalah* and insinuate that Ben Clifford was merely a figment of his own imagination and the works were his own!

I was outraged. As the true heir to the Master's work, I felt that I and I alone could explain it—for was I not the first and only initiate of our Order never to be sworn to secrecy? The Lord had struck our Master down in order that *I* might be allowed to speak the truth to the world about Rabbi Lamed Ben Clifford.

However, after reading DuQuette's lovingly respectful editing and introductions to the texts, I must confess he has done an admirable job. I certainly cannot fault him for exploiting his own celebrated status to bring the works of this great Qabalist to the general public.

And so, dear reader, here for the first time you have the Master's work in your hands. I cannot completely condone its provinance, though I bow to its magnificent simplicity of thought—a small but perfectly formed nugget of Qabalistic wisdom. I hope you enjoy it. In the words of the Master's favorite magical expression: V.I.T.R.I.O.L.!

—Rodney Orpheus
Los Angeles, California

INTRODUCTION
CONFESSION

by Lon Milo DuQuette

For hundreds of years a small but zealous number of orthodox[1] Jewish men have preserved a complex and highly structured tradition of study and meditation, based partly upon an intense analysis of the Hebrew scriptures and Talmudic texts, and partly upon the writings of several influential thinkers of the Medieval and Renaissance periods. These pious and dedicated Kabbalists[2] absorbed themselves passionately in a perpetual quest for the revealed word of God.

Parallel to this, for hundreds of years non-Jewish mystics have seized many of the tools of Qabalistic study and applied them to Christian,[3] heretical, magical[4] and, most recently, New Age paradigms. This latter group, while not discarding completely the fascination with the Hebrew and Christian scriptures, focuses primarily on the consciousness-expanding benefits derived from the practice of Qabalistic meditative exercises rather than the parochial revelations resulting from scriptural exegesis.

KABBALAH-CABALA-QABALAH

Understandably, orthodox *K*abbalists do not have much respect for *C*abalists and *Q*abalists, and, from their point of view, this snobbery is well justified. Nevertheless, it cannot be denied that great spiritual benefit can be derived from Qabalistic thought and exercise, even if the student chooses not to embrace the Hebrew religion, or make a spiritual commitment to traditions or articles of faith which may be incongruent or irrelevant to his or her spiritual worldview.

At the present time, disciples of the non-traditional Qabalah represent a much wider spectrum of seekers than that of the orthodox community. Included in this broad band of Qabalistic dabblers are mathematicians, physicists, psychologists, entertainers, as well as students and practitioners of the Western Hermetic traditions of esoteric Freemasonry, Tarot, Ceremonial Magick, Rosicrucianism, Astrology, and Alchemy. With all due homage and respect to the adepts and traditions of the orthodox Hebrew Kabbalah, it is to this larger group of *un*orthodox (or non-orthodox) Qabalists that this book is addressed.

QABALAH—FUNNY?

For the last twenty years I have attempted to introduce the Qabalah to students of Tarot and Ceremonial Magick, in particular to those who are interested in the work of the Golden Dawn and/or Aleister Crowley's Ordo Templi Orientis. The scope of this work is relatively narrow, and deals primarily with the meanings and numerical equivalents of the letters of the Hebrew alphabet, the mysteries of the schematic diagrams known as the "Tree of Life," and the "Cube of Space," and the various exercises with which the diligent student "connects everything in the universe with everything else until there is no 'anything' left."

Early on, I discovered that I could quickly convey the fundamentals by using simple anecdotes and metaphors. As the years progressed, these homespun tales have become increasingly colorful, outrageous and, in my humble opinion, quite amusing. Moreover, students and critics repeatedly tell me that they seem to absorb and retain the information more efficiently (and have a better chance of staying awake) when the material is presented to them in this manner.

When I began to organize the material for this book, I realized that the vast majority of readers would not be familiar with my personality and the subtle nuances of my comedic timing. I knew that, if I were to plunge the unsuspecting reader directly into the waters of my Qabalistic fairyland, the poor souls would immediately imagine themselves drowned in pure silliness. So I turned to a literary device that has a long and distinguished history in the world of Qabalistic literature—pseudepigraphy, or the ascription of false names of authors to certain works. Revered Hebrew scholar, Gershom G. Scholem wrote:

> For a long time we have known that literary forgeries repre-
> sent a flight into anonymity and pseudonymity just as often
> as they indicate trickery; and not for nothing have we
> retained the foreign word, "pseudepigrapha" to designate in
> particular a legitimate category of religious literature . . . the
> Zohar is the most important but by far not the only exam-
> ple of such love of masquerade in Jewish literature.[5]

I decided to do just what Rabbi Moshe de Leon did when he wrote the Zohar,[6] in the 13th century. He credited authorship to a fictitious holy man, Rabbi Shimon Ben Yohai, a second-century victim of the Roman persecution who, while hiding for thirteen years in a cave, was inspired by God to write the Zohar. Scholars may debate whether de Leon or a contemporary was actually the author of the Zohar, but none considers the text to be fraudulent in the ordinary sense of the word. It is obviously based on much older material and the practice of ascribing ancient authorship to documents was a common and accepted practice in those days. So why not today?

For my purposes I invented Rabbi Lamed Ben Clifford, leg-endary *l'enfant terrible* of the modern Qabalisitic movement. Ben Clifford has afforded me the opportunity to soar to outrageous (and hopefully) memorable heights and, when necessary, stand apart from the silliness to highlight the golden eggs of Qabalistic wisdom nested therein. This may smack a bit of schizophrenia, and I must admit I have enjoyed being the Rabbi's biographer and critic. I hope the reader will also be able to suspend his or her disbelief long enough to join in the fun and learn the fundamentals of the Qabalah.

While it is certainly not my intention to offend anyone with Rabbi Ben Clifford's escapades, it is perhaps inevitable that the format of this book will chafe the sensibilities of those who have forgotten that spiritual discovery can be a joyous experience and that great truths can be transmitted through the medium of laughter. To each and every one of you who finish this little book and still feel offended by its content or style, I offer you in advance my sincere and profound apology.

I also caution and rebuke all hatemongers and bigots whose dangerous pathologies and diseased minds would interpret my playful treatment of Jewish themes as being anything other than lovingly good-natured.

Now that's been said, I think it is time to sit back, suspend your disbelief and pretend for a few hours that Rabbi Lamed Ben Clifford is real. Listen carefully to what he has to say. I did—and now I'm proud to say, "Hell yes! I'm a Chicken Qabalist!"

O

WHO WAS
RABBI LAMED BEN CLIFFORD?

First of all, I feel I must apologize to the reader for the unusual format of this book. The raw material came from wildly varied sources and I confess my editing skills were severely challenged. With the exception of *The Ten Command-Rants and Commentary*, which appeared in the Winter 1989 issue of *Gomer* magazine, and his 1992 interview in *Augury Today* magazine, all of Ben Clifford's writings were unpublished and unedited. Several articles were written as lectures to the imaginary students of his equally imaginary "Zerubbabel Institute of Philosophical Youth," and others, like "Frequently Asked Questions about Chicken Qabalah," were compiled from letters written to students around the world. Arguably, the most unusual section of the book is the unedited screenplay text from his *Let's Learn Chicken Qabalah*, a never-produced video documentary. Try as I might, I was unable to translate this remarkable work into straight text without losing vitally important information provided by visual gimmicks and queues from the Rabbi's delightfully twisted imagination.

Before July 23, 1997, when his disciples reported him missing, Rabbi Lamed Ben Clifford was virtually unknown to the world of modern esotericism. The few individuals who knew of the man and his work were violently polarized in their opinions. Most dismissed him as a mad and impudent charlatan. A tiny number, however, passionately embraced his "Chicken Qabalah," and reveled in his irreverent and sometimes offensive style, proclaiming it "dust in the eyes of the profane."

There is no question about it, Ben Clifford was in many respects an unabashed phony. He was a fraud from the insipid propeller atop his yarmulke to the "talismanic" lifts in his shoes. He most certainly was *not* a bona fide Rabbi. Despite his protestations to the contrary, he held no academic degrees or certificates of rabbinical training. He was not the president of the Zerubbabel Institute of Philosophical Youth (Z.I.P.Y.), nor, to the best of my knowledge, has such an organization ever existed. His name was obviously bogus and those that knew of his passion for sweet-and-sour pork will confirm that he probably did not consider himself a practicing Jew.

On the other hand, it appears no one was ever harmed by Ben Clifford's chicanery. To my knowledge, he was never accused of any crime more serious than that of bad taste. No one has ever denied that he was extremely well-read, and that some time in his nebulous past he most certainly achieved deep and profound levels of spiritual illumination. Be that as it may, I did not write this book as a defense of this colorful eccentric, but to introduce the golden treasures of the man's thoughts to a broader audience.

I'm sure it will be apparent to the reader who is already well versed on the subject, that Ben Clifford's teachings are far from an exhausting exposition of the myriad (sometimes conflicting) doctrines of the Qabalah. For example, he omits altogether any discussion of the Qliphoth or the false Sephirah Daath. He also chose to adhere exclusively to the venerable, yet simplistic, doctrine of a four-part division of the soul, ignoring (at least in print) the more complex theories which posit a greater Neshamah subdivided into Neshamah-Chiah-Yechidah.[1]

However, I caution the adept reader against jumping to the conclusion that Ben Clifford's teachings in any way "dumbs-down" the

Qabalah. He has, in my opinion, accomplished the nearly impossible task of distilling to its essence one of the most (if not *the* most) complex spiritual sciences in the world. He offers the new student the opportunity to grasp the big Qabalistic picture before he or she feels obliged to start (as the Rabbi wrote) "counting the nostril hairs of God." At the same time, his unpretentious approach to the subject serves to remind the veteran Qabalist (who perhaps *has* been counting the nostril hairs of God for many years) that there is a big Qabalistic picture.

The last thirty years have witnessed a proliferation of interest in the occult and all aspects of the Western mystery tradition. There is no argument among the well-informed that the Hebrew Qabalah throbs at the very heart of this tradition, sometimes as the source, sometimes as the transmitter of the wisdom of the ages. To this new generation of seekers, some of whom may be destined to plumb the deepest mysteries of the Qabalah, and others who will be satisfied just to scratch the surface, I am honored to present *The Chicken Qabalah of Rabbi Lamed Ben Clifford.*

—Lon Milo DuQuette
Newport Beach, California

1

FREQUENTLY ASKED QUESTIONS ABOUT CHICKEN QABALAH

Introduced by Lon Milo DuQuette

We are Qabalists not to prove the Bible is holy—
we are Qabalists because everything *is holy.*
—RABBI LAMED BEN CLIFFORD

Without doubt, the first question people asked Rabbi Lamed Ben Clifford concerned his choice of the word "Chicken" to describe his brand of Qabalistic study and practice. It is clear to me, after reviewing scores of letters on this subject, that he delighted in giving a different answer to every individual who asked, "Why do you call it *Chicken* Qabalah?" Indeed, for this reason, I had altogether given up the idea of including any of them in the "Frequently Asked Questions" chapter. Then, shortly before returning the last draft of the manuscript to my publisher, I received a telephone call from one of the Rabbi's students living in New York City. She was a wealth of information and happily corroborated the following story, which was part of a 1987 letter to a Jamaican disciple.

> Why do I call it Chicken Qabalah? Actually, the term "Chicken Qabalah" issued from the mouth of an arrogant and hateful old man who attended my New York City

YOU-CAN-FORGET-90-PERCENT-OF-WHAT-YOU-KNOW-ABOUT-THE-QABALAH seminar. After my talk he approached me, so obviously infuriated that he could hardly speak.

He said, "Sir, you speak blaspheme! You are no Kabbalist! You don't even pronounce the word correctly—it is Kahb-bah-`law! Kahb-bah-`law! What you teach is not Kabbalah! It is...it is..."

The poor man's face turned bright red and his whole body began to shake as he searched his mind for a word *fowl* [*sic*] enough to describe my work.

"It is—it is—Chicken! Chicken Kahb-bah-`law!"

It was instantly obvious to everyone in the room that he was painfully embarrassed at the ill-chosen and infantile words that blurted mindlessly out of his mouth. People started to chuckle. He then became so flustered that he spat upon the floor and said, "You and your teachings merit only spit! Spit!" and then he stormed out of the hall.

As I am vowed to interpret every phenomenon as a direct communication from God to my soul, I recognized this awful slobbering man as an angel of the Lord, sent to reveal to me the name of the spiritual science that would forever cling to my name. That night in meditation I examined his message Qabalistically.

The Hebrew word for *phlegm* or *spittle* is כיח (KICh), and the word for *merit* is נה (NE). To my great joy, the phrase "merit spit," נה כיח, enumerates[1] to the number 93, one of the holiest of numbers. Number 93 relates not only to the divine concepts of Love and Will, but also to the great secret Word by which we triumph over death. I then looked down at my notes to discover that the very same letters arranged in the very same order rendered in English characters the word נה כ יח (ChI KEN).

I cannot say that I actually believe the above story. It might have some basis in fact, but, like most of the Rabbi's stories, it is probably pure fiction (or as he would say, "a Holy Whopper"). As we will soon see, however, the lies of Rabbi Lamed Ben Clifford can contain some very great truths.

The list of questions and answers, below, was not compiled by Ben Clifford. I compiled it with the kind help of his secretary and "magical son," Gizmo Ben Lamed, from nearly 6 years of the Rabbi's personal correspondence with disciples and detractors.

What is Chicken Qabalah?

Chicken Qabalah is the deceptively self-effacing term given to those aspects of the Holy Hebrew Qabalah that are of *practical* value to practitioners of the Western Hermetic spiritual tradition. While giving the most profound respect to individuals and institutions that teach the rich parochial traditions of speculative Qabalah, Chicken Qabalists, like students of Zen, focus pragmatically on the mind-transcending techniques of the art.

Who are Chicken Qabalists?

Anybody can be a Chicken Qabalist, but at this point in history most are students of Tarot, Psychology, Astrology, Ceremonial Magick, Rosicrucianism, Alchemy, Mystic Freemasonry, or Witchcraft."

Is Chicken Qabalah real Qabalah?

Hell yes! Don't worry about it, and don't let anyone tell you otherwise. So-called orthodox Qabalahs are only other people's Chicken Qabalahs that have been around for a long time.

Is there a correct way to spell the word Qabalah?

Hell no! You're a Chicken Qabalist! Don't worry about it. Cabala, Kabbalah, Quabbbalah, Caqubabalalah—They're all wrong! (So they may as well all be correct!) We'll talk about that more when you are a little more familiar with the Hebrew alphabet.

Is it hard to become a Chicken Qabalist?

Hell no! Don't worry about it. But, if you feel you need some external validation, sign this, cut it out and put it in your wallet. No need to send in an application or pay any dues. If the omniscient Deity really exists, It will surely recognize your bold act of spiritual audacity.

Zerrubbabel Institute of Philosophical Youth
Z.I.P.Y.
This is to certify that

_____

wallows guiltlessly in the nonsectarian freedom of thought
exemplified in the Mystical Science of the
Chicken Qabbalah of
Rabbi Lamed Ben Clifford

and because of that act of intelligence and good taste is
entitled to the honor and respect of all self-assured and
unpretentious seekers of truth everywhere, and forever is
entitled to bear the august title of

CHICKEN QABALIST

"Hell no! I don't worry about it!"

Figure 1. Wallet card for the Chicken Qabalist.

There! You're a full-fledged Chicken Qabalist. Now, the first thing you need to learn is that everyone's Qabalah is uniquely their own. Your Qabalah is not my Qabalah or anyone else's. A personal Qabalah is placed in your hands the moment you take up the study. It's alive, and grows upon what you feed it. The more you learn, the more you use. No two students study or work the same.

For example: I know people who have studied most, if not all, of the classic texts. They know their Hebrew backward and forward, and a whole poop-load of the traditional correspondences. They can twist and abuse numbers and letters all night long and send you out the door screaming with their nonstop raving. They can manipulate your address and phone number to prove you're the antichrist, and your real name is Rumplestiltskin. However, all that doesn't necessarily mean they are using that knowledge to do anything other than bore their friends to death. On the other hand, you might be inclined to learn and use only one or two Qabalistic tricks of the trade. That's fine. Used everyday with tenacity and skill, even the most elementary exercises can drive you crazy just as fast as the complex and exotic operations—maybe faster! Don't worry about it!

Do I need to be Jewish?

Hell no! You're a Chicken Qabalist! Don't worry about it. You don't need to be born anything, believe anything, or belong to any religion, cult, order, or political party. You don't need to believe in the Hebrew God, or Moses, or the Great Goddess, or Jesus, or L. Ron Hubbard, or Mohammed, or any other savior, prophet, or salesperson. You don't even need a faithful heart or an open mind. The brain-warping power of Qabalistic thought will soon make all those things irrelevant.

Will I need to learn the Hebrew language?

Hell no! You're a Chicken Qabalist! Don't worry about it. You don't have to learn to speak Hebrew. But you will have to recognize and be able to write the 22 letters of the Hebrew alphabet. You will also have to know the meanings and the numerical values of each Hebrew letter.[2] There is no escaping this part of your education. Eventually, as you study and work with the alphabet, you will become familiar with various Hebrew words that are important to the system.

Soon, if your studies take you in that direction, you will be able to recognize these words in the original Hebrew texts. This skill is very impressive to friends and relatives who always thought you were stupid and unspiritual. Best of all, it will make them feel guilty and have agonizing doubts about their own religious beliefs because they can't read their own scriptures in the original tongue. Go ahead. Rub it in! Being a Chicken Qabalist is fun!

Won't I be intimidated by serious Jewish Qabalists and others who speak Hebrew?

Hell no! You're a Chicken Qabalist! Don't worry about it. The first liberating secret Chicken Qabalists learn is that (as far as the Qabalah is concerned) *there is no such thing as correct Hebrew pronunciation!*[3] Yep! That's right. No matter how you pronounce the various words in the system, some snob is sure to pop up (especially in public) and correct you. Remember that Hebrew, as a spoken language is relatively young. Sure, there are those who speak Yiddish, or Judezmo, Sephardic, or Ashkenazic, and a score of other regional and ethnic dialects. There *are* correct ways to pronounce these dialects, but nobody, I repeat, nobody knows for sure what the sacred language of the ancient Hebrews sounded like, or even if it was spoken at all! Pronunciation has less than nothing to do with the study and practical spiritual applications of the Qabalah.

Be proud of the fact that you are informed and honest enough to admit you are not sure how the words are pronounced and, what's more, you don't even care. Such crass indifference is unbearable to those who would dare belittle the work of the Chicken Qabalist.

That being said, it's always a good idea to remember:

> *Rabbi Lamed's Helpful Hint Number 1:* Never correct other Qabalists' pronunciation of Hebrew words no matter how silly it sounds. First of all, they might be right. Secondly, your silence will make them think you are a highly intelligent person because you agree with them.

> *Rabbi Lamed's Helpful Hint Number 2:* Better still, just don't talk with other Qabalists.

I hear the Qabalah is based on the Bible. Do I have to believe in the Bible?

Hell no! You're a Chicken Qabalist! Don't worry about it. You don't have to believe in anything. If the Bible leaves a bad taste in your mouth, welcome to the club. But before you throw old King James out the window, I'd like to point out that the Bible *is* holy—but so are the phonebook, Webster's Dictionary, Robert's Rules of Order and the menu at McDonalds. As you will learn from the Ten Command-Rants,[4] everything is holy and anything is capable of being the vehicle of divine revelation. Key books of the Bible, however, were written *by* Qabalists *for* Qabalists and so should be of particular interest to us.

I know, you're probably not thrilled about Bible study. Perhaps like me you've had unpleasant experiences with people who are convinced that the Bible teaches the most ridiculous and monstrous things. Well, now you can tell all those spiritual bullies who tried to terrorize you with the eternal agonies of hell that they can just go there. I'm going to share a little secret with you that only Chicken Qabalists (and a few musicians) have the courage and wit to handle: *The people who wrote the Qabalistic books of the Bible never intended for them to be read by the public.*

There! I've said it. I feel so much better. Be honest with yourself. Deep in your heart, you've always known it was true, haven't you?

How many times have you tried to wade into Genesis or Ezekiel, and finally just gave up and said, "What the hell are these guys talking about?" Don't feel bad. You weren't meant to know what they're talking about—not unless you held vital interpretive keys.

I know that sounds snobby and elitist, but it's the truth. These texts were crafted by mystics possessed of profound understanding of the universe and the mysteries of human existence. At a time when writing was reserved for priests and royalty, they used poetry and parables to express thoughts that everyday language could not accommodate. They assembled the phrases with great art from individual words that conveyed an even deeper level of truth; and finally, each word was made up of unique symbolic letters, each of which revealed yet another story—a story so profound and abstract it could only be told and understood in the pure language of numbers and mathematics.

These sages were full-time holy guys. They wrote this stuff for other full-time holy guys, and the tiny segment of every generation who would be equipped with the intelligence, the spiritual drive (and leisure time) necessary to embark upon a lifelong quest for enlightenment. I assure you, these ancient mystics would have produced a radically different body of work had they in their wildest nightmares imagined that in some future dark age their secret coded scriptures would be seized by half-witted and sadistic European cannibals and interpreted literally, like some grotesque and racist history book.

Will the study of the Qabalah make me a better person?

No! You'll have to do that yourself.

2

THE TEN COMMAND-RANTS

Introduced by Lon Milo DuQuette

Don't worry if none of this makes any sense to you right now.
It is enough to remember that Realization *of One is the*
second-to-last goal of all Qabalists. The final goal is
to attain the consciousness *of Nothing.*
—RABBI LAMED BEN CLIFFORD

R abbi Ben Clifford claimed that in the winter of 1989 he made a pilgrimage to the Holy Land, where he climbed Mount Sinai to, as he put it, "touch base and get further clarification" on several matters pertaining to scripture. On the summit, the Supreme Deity allegedly appeared to him in the form of a rotating tongue sandwich that lectured Ben Clifford for about six minutes. To quote the Rabbi:

> *The Lord's lustrous lingua lashed from the luminous laser-like*
> *lights that licked the length of the lush and lonely landscape.*
> *Later, I laughed like a lunatic as I lay lifelessly limp and lin-*
> *gered upon the lilt of the last littlest letter of the Laws and the*
> *laudable lessons I so lately learned.*

Of course this story is a complete fabrication. To my knowledge, Ben Clifford never visited Israel, and in 1989 would have been physically unfit to climb any mountain. In fact, I have spoken to several of his early students, who informed me that in the winter of 1989 the

Rabbi was hospitalized in New York City after suffering an emotional breakdown on the observation deck of the Empire State Building after becoming violently ill at the Carnegie Deli.

Be that as it may, the fact remains that in late 1989 Ben Clifford did indeed publish a short treatise on the nature of the creation and the underlying theory of Qabalistic study. These "Ten Command-Rants," as he called them, are a work of unquestioned genius. They are perhaps the most concise description of the nature of reality ever penned, reducing complex and inscrutable concepts to their essence. Their publication in the prestigious Qabalah magazine, *Gomer*, resulted in Rabbi Ben Clifford's overnight transformation from crazy-old-burned-out lunatic to crazy-old-burned-out-lunatic holy man.

I consider his subsequent commentaries on the Ten Command-Rants the best introduction to the Qabalah ever written. They continue to be, for me, a perpetual reminder of why I am on the great Qabalistic adventure. I strongly advise the student to refer to them often throughout the years of his or her mystical career.

The Ten Command-Rants

COMMENTARIES ON
THE TEN COMMAND-RANTS

First Command-Rant
All is One.

This statement is hardly a veil-rending revelation to anyone who has dabbled even slightly with abstract thought. It's easy to imagine everything in the universe lumped together into one big *something* beyond which there is nothing. But it's the concept of nothing that sends our primate minds into a tailspin. Now, the very young Chicken Qabalist might be tempted to think of this divine nothingness as kind of a negative "enO" from which the "One" somehow popped into being as if from behind a mysterious looking-glass. But, as the Second Command-Rant will demonstrate, "nothing" is "something else" altogether.

Second Command-Rant
The First Command-Rant is a lie. All is Nothing.

Astronomers and physicists tell us there is more nothing in the universe than anything else. In fact, they now say that most of the matter and energy in the cosmos (well over 90 percent) is somehow hiding in all this nothingness. Come to think about it, even matter that

TEN COMMAND-RANTS

I. ALL IS ONE.

II. THE FIRST COMMAND-RANT
IS A LIE. ALL IS NOTHING.

III. THERE REALLY ISN'T A
CREATION, TIME, OR SPACE,
HEAVEN OR EARTH...BUT
THERE IS A YOU.

IV. WE PERCEIVE THERE IS A
CREATION, TIME, AND SPACE,
HEAVEN AND EARTH BECAUSE
OF A FUNDAMENTAL DEFECT
IN OUR POWERS OF PERCEPTION.

V. THIS DEFECT CANNOT BE REPAIRED,
BUT IT CAN BE OVERCOME.

JB 222

TEN COMMAND-RANTS

VI. IN ORDER TO OVERCOME OUR DEFECTIVE POWERS OF PERCEPTION WE MUST BE WILLING TO ABUSE THEM UNTIL THEY BREAK.

VII. EVERTHING IN HEAVEN AND EARTH IS CONNECTED TO EVERYTHING IN HEAVEN AND EARTH.

VIII. EVERYTHING IN HEAVEN AND EARTH IS THE REFLECTION OF EVERYTHING IN HEAVEN AND EARTH.

IX. EVERYTHING IN HEAVEN AND EARTH CONTAINS THE PATTERN OF EVERYTHING IN HEAVEN AND EARTH.

X. LOOK HARD ENOUGH AT ANYTHING AND YOU WILL EVENTUALLY SEE EVERYTHING.

JB 222

we can see is really mostly nothing. There is infinitely more nothing in an atom than protons and electrons. There is more nothing in our bodies than anything else. We are full of tubes and pockets and sacs and bladders and cavities and chambers and openings and voids. Every cell in your body is mostly nothing. When a cell starts to divide to produce more cells, it first folds in on itself to create more precious nothing to work with. Even your brain grew out of the nothingness of this embryonic internal disappearing act.

Physicists cannot even say with any certainty that matter, as most people think of it, exists at all. The components of atoms (protons, neutrons, electrons, quarks, charm, etc.) are not matter. They are tendencies. (Tell that to your head the next time you slam it getting into your car!) Physicists and mystics are now using the same vocabulary, and it is only a matter of time before our learned men and women of science will announce clearly what Qabalists have been saying cryptically for centuries.

Elements of creation as we know them—minerals and metals, animals and people, planets and stars, light and energy—are merely the husks of an invisible universal force that sustains the entire cosmos. We're like dead skin cells that have flaked off from the body of the unmanifest Super-Being. This force—this nothingness, is better than reality. It is undiluted, unlimited potentiality! It is the ultimate reality, and the nature of that reality is pure consciousness.

The first thing that attracted me to the Qabalah as a young Chicken Qabalist (hatchling) was the concept that everything proceeded out of this "Nothing." That made Nothing the ultimate creator, not the Elohim,[1] or Jehovah, or any of the other ill-tempered bullies of the Old Testament. I liked the idea of brooding and inscrutable Nothing behind everything in the universe.

You can *think* about the Elohim creating stuff like crazy; you can *think* about YHVH Elohim[2] blowing life into Adam's nose; you can even think about a sneaky stinky cloud killing the first-born babies in ancient Egypt; but you can't *think* about Nothing! Anything you can think about —anything you can capture and hold in your mind's eye—is automatically disqualified from infinityhood and can't possibly be the ultimate Deity.

Qabalistic tradition informs us that everything proceeded from the Great One, and the Great One proceeded from a very special kind of Nothing—actually three very special kinds of Nothing. Beginning Chicken Qabalists need not spend a great deal of time trying to grasp this concept because, first, it can't be understood, and second, if you did understand it, there would no longer be a need for you to study anything. However, as you approach the meditative summit of your career as a Chicken Qabalist, the irrational mystery of the three kinds of Nothing will increasingly absorb you. For this reason I offer the following.

The first kind of Nothing is called Ain אין.[3] This Nothing is really nothing—not even the concept of no-thing (i.e., the absence of anything). Now, if Ain just sat around nowhere doing nothing it's a sure bet that nothing was going to get done. However, something happened to make Ain actually *become* Nothing (maybe because it was Nothing all along and just had to wake up to the fact). This new, defined Nothing the Qabalists call Limitless Nothing, or Ain Soph אין סוף. The third kind of Nothing is a hybrid Ain Soph called Ain Soph Aur, אין סוף אור, Limitless Light. I view it as the light bulb that goes off in the vastness of Ain Soph when it realizes the perfect Notness of its Nothingness! Nothing is Not! This double negative is tantamount to saying "Something is!" and sets the stage for the first Positive in the universe—the concept of One.[4]

Don't worry if none of this makes any sense to you right now. It is enough to remember that *realization* of "One" is the second-to-last goal of all Qabalists. The final goal is to attain the *consciousness* of "Nothing."

Third Command-Rant
There really isn't a creation, time or space, Heaven or Earth . . .

Get used to it. Ultimate reality is Nothing, so all perceivable phenomena, including time and space, are illusions. We could take a picture proving this if our camera had a wide enough lens. That lens, of course, would have to take in not only the absolute One, but all that Nothing, too!

Third Command-Rant *(continued)*
. . . But there is a you!

On the other hand, *you* are real[5]—a sparkling image of the absolute reality. You must remember, however, that the real you is something far different and more wonderful than your ape-like brain and reptilian nervous system can grasp. The real you is not just a piece of the force of universal consciousness—the real you is, in essence, the universal consciousness itself! You are not your body, or your brain, or your mind, or your astral body, or any of the more subtle sheathes that yogis and spoon-benders say you are nestled inside. Bodies and brains and minds are as unreal as creation, time, space, Heaven or Earth. The real you doesn't eat, or drink, or think, or sleep, or die. I'm sure we would all be amazed to know just how skinny, and light, and thoughtless, and sleepless, and immortal we really are.

Fourth Command-Rant
We perceive there is a creation, time and space, Heaven, and Earth because of a fundamental defect in our powers of perception.

Our eyes cannot see infrared or ultraviolet; our ears cannot hear a dog-whistle or the extra-low frequencies generated by giant redwood trees; most people's noses can't even smell the difference between Coke and Pepsi. Even if we could utilize all the sensitive new scientific instruments that enable us to see more, hear more, or smell more, do we really think that we could ever gather enough information (or develop powers of intelligence profound enough to interpret that information) to unveil the ultimate reality? Get real! We are all sleepwalkers stumbling blind, deaf, and numb through a life we could never understand even if we could see, hear, feel, or smell like Superman.

It is perfectly natural for you to ask, "Why is there evil in the world?" or "Why do bad things happen to good people?" but stop flattering yourself. You're never going to find an answer to those questions by gathering information with your senses and attempting to process that information with your brain.

Fifth Command-Rant
This defect cannot be repaired, but it can be overcome.

Caution: Most people will be happier if they never try to overcome this defect. That is why most people in the world find it so easy to believe the most outrageous religious concepts without batting an eyelash. The rest of us brave and foolish souls must consciously misuse our defective powers of perception to our advantage. This is done by Qabalistic study and thought.

Sixth Command-Rant
In order to overcome our defective powers of perception we must be willing to abuse them until they break.

Qabalistic study and thought is designed to make you crazier than most people by requiring that you attain the all-encompassing consciousness of the real you. Obviously, this is not easy to achieve, but you may as well bite the bullet and get to work because it is the ultimate fate of all units of evolving consciousness—even Chicken Qabalists!

In order to hit this mystical and omniscient mark, it will be necessary for you to partially disable the mechanisms of normal thought by overloading your laughably inadequate mind with data from your laughably inadequate powers of perception. If all goes well, you will become so sick of the whole ponderous cosmos that your inadequate faculties will look for any way out of the insanity and eventually surrender to transcendent consciousness.[6]

The first step is easy. All you have to do is join 99 percent of the world's population and accept creation/time/space/Heaven/Earth as "reality." Then, through Qabalistic exercises, you systematically dissect and analyze every aspect of that "reality." You connect everything you can think of with everything else you can think of until there is no "anything" left.

This process is not as tedious as it may at first appear because the illusionary universe obligingly provides us with three very helpful Command-Rants of its own.

- Everything in Heaven and Earth is *connected* to everything in Heaven and Earth.

- Everything in Heaven and Earth is the *reflection* of everything in Heaven and Earth.

- Everything in Heaven and Earth *contains the pattern* of everything in Heaven and Earth.

Seventh Command-Rant
Everything in Heaven and Earth is connected to everything in Heaven and Earth.

This one's easy. We are living in a wall-to-wall universe. Everything is connected to everything else. The lox on the cream cheese rests upon the bagel; which is connected to my fingers; which are connected to my hand; which is connected (via the rest of my body) to my foot; which is connected to my shoe; which is connected to the floor; which is part of the delicatessen; which rests upon Earth; which is spinning in space; which also contains and is connected to the Sun, the Moon, the stars, and all the other heavenly bodies in the universe.

It follows, then, that all lox is ultimately connected to all cream cheese, bagels, fingers, hands, feet, shoes, floors, delicatessens, planets, Sun, Moon, stars and heavenly bodies everywhere. It also follows that each unit of lox possesses a special affinity with every other unit of lox by virtue of its vibratory "*lox*ness," and by the fact that they are all indirectly connected. Naturally, the same can be said for all cream cheese, bagels, body parts, and extraterrestrial delicatessens.

Eighth Command-Rant
Everything in Heaven and Earth is the reflection of everything in Heaven and Earth.

A piano has 88 keys, but theoretically we could build a piano with an infinite number of keys stretching forever lower in one direction and forever higher in the other. But no matter how big we make our piano, we will never have more than twelve notes with which to play. We can draw similar parallels in the characteristics of light and color, and the behavior of organic and mineral life.

In the subatomic realm, electrons orbit the nucleus of the atom in the same way moons orbit their planets, and planets orbit stars, and solar systems orbit whatever inscrutable "thing" is at the center of their galaxies, etc.

Look around. You are smack dab in the middle of a ribbon of repeating patterns stretching infinitely toward macrocosmic immensity in one direction, and infinitely toward microcosmic smallness in the other. As above, so below. If we study the tiny subject, we simultaneously study its giant counterpart and vice versa.

Nineth Command-Rant
Everything in Heaven and Earth contains the pattern of everything in Heaven and Earth.

This Command-Rant is really an extension of the previous one. As everything in Heaven and Earth is the reflection of everything in Heaven and Earth, every reflect*ee* houses a faithful blueprint of that which it reflects. Since prehistoric times, this was observable in flora and fauna, but now we are magically blessed with the wondrous knowledge of DNA. Not only does everything in Heaven and Earth contain the pattern of everything in Heaven and Earth, everything is first cousin to everything in Heaven and Earth!

Tenth Command-Rant
Look hard enough at anything and you will eventually see everything.

Only then, dear Chicken Qabalist, will you have an eye big enough to really close . . . so you can finally get some well-deserved rest.

3

THE SEPHER YETZIRAH

Introduced by Lon Milo DuQuette

What happened to Jehovah? Isn't Jehovah God?
Didn't Jehovah create Heaven and Earth? Hell no!
Elohim did, and Elohim is a very peculiar word.
—RABBI LAMED BEN CLIFFORD

The Qabalah is not a book. There are, however many texts which form the literary foundation of Qabalistic study. A rather extensive bibliography can be found at the end of this book. Of primary interest to fledgling Chicken Qabalists is the Sepher Yetzirah or Book of Formation. This work is ascribed to the patriarch Abraham (but, to quote Rabbi Ben Clifford, "That's a crock!"). Nevertheless, the Sepher Yetzirah is very old—perhaps the oldest philosophical treatise written in Hebrew.[1]

There are three important features that make the Sepher Yetzirah particularly attractive to the lazy and pretentious. First of all (and most importantly) it is very short and relatively easy to understand. Second, it introduces us to the concept of the 10 Sephiroth, or Emanations that emerge from the primal unity. In later Qabalistic literature the concept of the 10 Sephiroth develops into the Tree of Life, a very helpful schematic, especially for Chicken Qabalists.[2]

Third, it tells the simple story of how Deity created the Hebrew alphabet then used the letters to form the words that brought the universe into being. This concept may sound a little silly, but this silliness is the foundation of the Qabalistic worldview and meditative exercises that will eventually obsess the diligent student.

Now, I am putting you on your honor to obtain at least one of the classic translations of the Sepher Yetzirah and put it in a conspicuous spot on your bookshelf. If you are a serious student you will most certainly wish to read it. But I warn you, even the best translations will appear very strange—full of tiresome and seemingly irrelevant ramblings. I confess that as a young student, I lamented the fact that, even though the Sepher Yetzirah was short, all the really useful information was buried under piles of archaic language and stupid-sounding redundancies. Imagine my great joy when I was introduced to Ben Clifford's marvelous and practical "translation."

Naturally, like all of the Rabbi's works, the text is surrounded by controversy. Ben Clifford swore to his students this version of the Sepher Yetzirah was a faithful translation of the most ancient and authoritative manuscript available, but there is no doubt that this is another one of his pathetic and transparent lies. The work is obviously a modern counterfeit. (The text even carelessly makes references to pizza and the theme music from the television game show "Jeopardy.") One of the Rabbi's students, who asked to remain anonymous, told me he believed the Rabbi himself concocted the "translation" in 1983 while recovering from a bout of Montezuma's revenge in a motel room in Ensenada, Mexico.

Be that as it may, like his Ten Command-Rants, Ben Clifford's treatment of the Sepher Yetzirah cuts straight to the heart of what Chicken Qabalists need to learn first. I do not hesitate to reprint the entire text, including his provocative introduction written to the students of his imaginary institute.

The Sepher Yetzirah

An Address by
Rabbi Lamed Ben Clifford
to the Students and Faculty of the
Zerubbabel Institute of Philosophical Youth

ויאמר אלהים יהי אור ויהי אור.

And said the Elohim, Let there be light: and there was light.
—Genesis 1:3

I'M SURE MANY OF YOU students are asking yourselves why I am starting our study of Genesis with the third verse of chapter 1 instead of the first. The answer is simple. Verse 1 tells us squat! It informs us; "In the beginning the Elohim created Heaven and Earth."[3]

Big deal! What the hell is an Elohim? Is it God? Translators of the English Bible seem to think so. Most versions read: "In the beginning *God* created Heaven and Earth."

What happened to Jehovah? Isn't Jehovah God? Didn't Jehovah create Heaven and Earth? Hell no! Elohim did, and Elohim is a very peculiar word.

El (אל)[4] is the root word for Deity. *Eloh* (אלה) is a feminine singular, in other words, a female Deity (a Goddess); *im* (ים) is the plural ending for things that are masculine. *Elohim* (אלהים), then, should be translated either "Gods and Goddesses" or "Dual-Gendered

Deity." Later on in verses 26 and 27 the Elohim even refer to themselves as plural, "And said the Elohim, Let *us* make Adam in *our* image, after *our* likeness: and let them have dominion over the fish of the sea, and over the fowl of the air, and over the cattle, and over all the Earth, and over every creeping thing that creepeth upon the Earth. And created the Elohim Adam in the image of Elohim created they them, male and female created they them."

Surprised? So was everyone who had their hearts set on God not having a vagina and everyone who believed that Adam was an historical character, like General Custer, and not just a name for the human race. They were so upset when they discovered *that in the beginning the Dual-Gendered Deity created Heaven and Earth* that they made sure that Elohim and innumerable other special names would be translated "God" or "Lord" or "Lord God" or other such ambiguous masculine-sounding names.[5]

Besides this little titbit, verse 1 leaves us in the dark concerning what Heaven is, what Earth is, or how the Elohim went about creating these things. Verse 2 is even worse:

> *And the Earth was without form, and void; and darkness was upon the face of the deep. And the Spirit of Elohim moved upon the face of the waters.*

If Earth was void and formless, where was all this water coming from? If the author was trying to be inscrutable, he sure did a damned good job of it.

Verse 3 finally gives us something we can dig our teeth into:

> *And the Elohim said, Let there be light: and there was light.*

The key word here is "said." That's how everything was created—the Elohim *talked* everything into existence.[6] The Elohim *said* it, and it was so. Obviously words are very important in the grand creation scenario. A word is a vibration, and vibration creates and sustains the universe. The atomic weight of the chemical elements is just another way of measuring their vibration. Molecules hold themselves together and bond with other molecules by the "glue" of their compatible vibrations. That's what is meant by the term "the creative Logos, or Word." That's what John[7] was talking about when he wrote, "In the beginning was the Word, and the Word was with God, and the Word was God." Duh!

And what, my sleepy students, are words made up of? Letters! Our Hebrew alphabet (and what other alphabet would the Elohim dare use?) is made up of 22 sacred letters, and the story of their creation is not found in the Bible, but in a mysterious little masterpiece called the Sepher Yetzirah: The Book of Formation.

Several years ago, I personally had the extraordinary good fortune of being allowed to purchase the earliest known manuscript of this sacred work from a mysterious street vendor just outside of Hussan's Cantina in Ensenada, Mexico. I painstakingly translated it by carefully copying the Hebrew characters into my personal computer using the standard Hebrew fonts included in my word processing program. When I finished, I simply selected the entire text and globally changed the font to Times New Roman. To my amazement it translated exactly as you see it. A Qabalistic miracle.

Sepher Yetzirah
The Book of Formation

PROLOGUE

Deity, whom we call Yah, Yea-man, Jehovah of hosts, Joe Heavy, What-It-Is, the Big Kahuna, the Mighty Duh, the living Elohim, King of the Universe, Omnipotent, All-King and Merciful, Supreme, and Extolled is all-powerful, eternal; who is really, really holy and very, very large; who is so big It is both King *and* Queen of the Universe, who is so all-encompassing and huge that It has nowhere to sit down because all the chairs are inside of Itself; who, because It is everywhere and nowhere, everything and nothing, had no one to play with—this Dude of Dudes created the Universe (with the help of three imaginary friends, "Numbers, Letters, and Words") in 32 Mysterious Paths of Wisdom. They consist of 10 Sephiroth out of nothing and of 22 Letters.

The Deity divided the 22 Letters into three divisions: Three Mothers (fundamental letters), Seven Double letters, and Twelve Simple letters.

THE 10 SEPHIROTH OUT OF NOTHING

Ten of these paths came out of nothing. (Because the Deity is everything, It had lots of nothing to play with.) These ten paths are called Sephiroth or emanations. Because they came out of nothing they aren't actually real. (But then, of course, only the Deity knows that for sure.)

The 10 Sephiroth out of nothing are reflected in the human body by our ten fingers and toes, five on each side. In between the two sets of fingers is the tongue, and in between the two sets of toes are the naughty bits that make humans creative beings, too—just like the Deity!

Ten are the Sephiroth not 9; 10 and not 11 or 12, or 6 ⅞. Think about that for a while. Inquire into it. Put it in your pipe and smoke it. Ponder it while the music from "Jeopardy" plays, and roll it around in your mouth a little before swallowing. Render it evident and lead the Creator back to Its throne so we can all go home.

But—at the same time, don't talk about it. Don't even think about it. If your mouth urges you to speak, burn its roof with hot pizza! If your heart urges you to think about it, turn on the television! As it is written, "Your answer must be in the form of a question."

Then 10 Sephiroth out of nothing are infinite in ten ways (I'll put them in Tree of Life order):

1. Beginning Infinite

3. Good Infinite   2. End Infinite

5. Height Infinite   4. Evil Infinite

6. Depth Infinite

8. West Infinite   7. East Infinite

9. North Infinite

10. South Infinite

Then 10 Sephiroth out of nothing appear like a lightning flash. Being endless, the Deity's word is in them when they go and return. They run like hell when the Deity orders them around, and are constantly groveling before the throne.

From the Spirit of the Living God (1) emanated Air (2), from the Air emanated Water (3), from the Water emanated Fire or Æther (4), from the Æther emanated the Height (5), and the Depth (6), the East (7), and the West (8), the North (9), and the South (10).

THE 22 LETTERS

The remaining twenty-two paths are the 22 letters of the Hebrew alphabet. They form the foundation of everything we can think of, and all the other things that will never occur to us. The Deity weighed them and measured them, poked them and prodded them, issued them numbers, stapled and two-hole punched them; stamped their passports and organized them, according to all the crazy sounds It could make with Its infinite and eternal mouth. Formed by the breath of Air, It fixed them on five places in the mouth: the Throat, the Palate, the Tongue, the Teeth, and the Lips.

The Deity divided the 22 letters into three divisions: Three Mothers or Fundamental Letters, Seven Doubles, and Twelve Simple Consonants.

THE THREE MOTHERS

Three are the Fundamental Letters. Three not four, not sixteen, not even 3.14159. Think about that real hard. Turn it over in your mind. Put it in the blender and hit puree. Render it evident and put a fresh battery in the pacemaker of the Most High.

The Three Fundamental Letters —ש מ א—(Aleph, Mem, Shin) are real Mothers and are extremely cool. Deity took their temperatures and tissue samples, and measured their cholesterol levels, issued them numbers, certified them, and formed by them lots of things, such as the breast, body, and head, and Heaven, Earth, and the atmosphere, and heat, cold, and moistness—but who cares about that stuff!

First and foremost, they represent the Three Primitive Elements in the universe and the spheres of consciousness those elements represent—Air (א Aleph), Water (מ Mem), and Fire (ש Shin).[8]

The Three Fundamental Letters—ש מ א—(Aleph, Mem, Shin) are also the Three Famous Dimensional Twins who, because of their amazing ability to stretch themselves to infinity, create the cosmic elbow room in which the entire universe manifests. Their names are: א Aleph—Updown, מ Mem—Eastwest, and ש Shin—Northsouth. Dost thou get this? Needest thou a picture? Then behold figure 3.

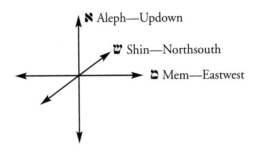

Figure 3. The Three Famous Dimensional Twins.

THE 7 DOUBLE LETTERS

The Double Letters are 7. Seven not 8, not 6 or F10. Hoist them up your flagpole. Clear your palate with them. Spay or neuter them, and spring for the Creator's bail.

The 7 Double Letters—ת ר פ כ ד ג ב—(Beth, Gimel, Daleth, Kaph, Peh, Resh, Tau) are rather confused and can be pronounced in a hard way and in a soft way. Because they can't make up their minds, they symbolize seven opposites: Life-Death, Peace-War, Wisdom-Folly, Wealth-Poverty, Beauty-Ugliness, Fruitfulness-Sterility, and Dominion-Slavery.

The 7 Double Letters also stand for the six dimensions (that were created when the Three Famous Dimensional Twins did their act and stretched themselves out). ב Beth for Above, ג Gimel for Below, ד Daleth for East, כ Kaph for West, פ Peh for North, ר Resh for South, and the hardworking ת Tau stands in the center and holds the whole thing together. Wilt thou need us to draw you another picture? Lookest to figure 4 (page 34).

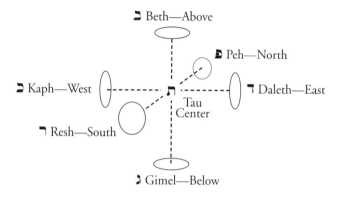

Figure 4. The Center and Six Dimensions.

The 7 Double Letters also stand for lots of other things, such as days of the week, and nostril holes, and other body openings. But who cares about that stuff! First and foremost, they represent the seven planets in the solar system, and the spheres of consciousness those planets represent: ב Beth for Mercury, ג Gimel for the Moon, ד Daleth for Venus, כ Kaph for Jupiter, פ Peh for Mars, ר Resh for the Sun, and ת Tau for Saturn.[9]

THE TWELVE SIMPLE LETTERS

Twelve are the Simple Letters. Twelve not 11, not—oh, you get the picture. Send out a memo. Brush and floss. Shampoo and fluff dry them, and rewrite the Creator's permanent record.

The twelve Simple Letters—ה ו ז ח ט י ל נ ס ע צ ק—(Heh, Vau, Zain, Cheth, Teth, Yod, Lamed, Nun, Samekh, Ayin, Tzaddi, and Qoph) are attributed to the oblique points, or edges, that were created when the six dimensions (that were created when the Three Famous Dimensional Twins did their act) were sealed and ran into each other at right angles: ה Heh, North East; ו Vau, South East; ז Zain, East Above; ח Cheth, East Below; ט Teth, North Above; י Yod, North Below; ל Lamed, North West; נ Nun, South West;

ꞇ Samekh, West Above; ע Ayin, West Below; צ Tzaddi, South Above; ק Qoph, South Below. Art thou following this? Wilt thou need another picture? See thou figure 5.

The Twelve Simple Letters also stand for lots of other things, such as months of the year, eggs in a carton, organs in the human body—but who cares!

First and foremost they represent the twelve constellations—the twelve signs of the zodiac—and the spheres of consciousness those twelve signs represent: ה Heh, Aries; ו Vau, Taurus; ז Zain, Gemini; ח Cheth, Cancer; ט Teth, Leo; י Yod, Virgo; ל Lamed, Libra; נ Nun, Scorpio; ס Samekh, Sagittarius; ע Ayin, Capricorn; צ Tzaddi, Aquarius; ק Qoph, Pisces.

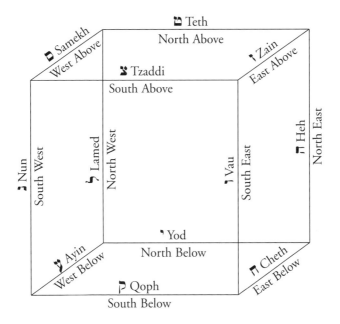

Figure 5. The Twelve Edges. Created by the Center and the Six Dimensions after the Three Dimensional Twins did their stretching act.

So endeth the Sepher Yetzirah. If this isn't enough information to keep you occupied for the rest of your life, then thou hast too much time on thine hands!

—Hecho en México

4

THE HEBREW ALPHABET

Introduced by Lon Milo DuQuette

ת *Tau looks like a* ר *Resh holding a dead dolphin by the tail.*
—RABBI LAMED BEN CLIFFORD

There's no escaping it. Even the laziest Chicken Qabalist needs to learn the Hebrew alphabet and at least some of its traditional correspondences.[1] As Rabbi Ben Clifford said in "Frequently Asked Questions," this doesn't mean that you will have to learn, speak, or read the Hebrew language. In fact, once you have learned the Hebrew alphabet and its Qabalistic and numerical secrets, you will most likely spend a lot of time examining English words and letters using their Hebrew equivalents.

Another thing that is absolutely necessary for your study is a small basic library of reference works. You don't have to have these books right now, but you will want them very soon. Of course you will collect more books as you descend into Qabalistic madness, but these texts (and this book, of course) will be enough to get you on the road:

Aleister Crowley, *777 and Other Qabalistic Writings* (York Beach, ME: Samuel Weiser 1990);

David Godwin, *Godwin's Cabalistic Encyclopedia* (St. Paul: Llewellyn, 1994);

Ehud Ben Yehuda, *Ben-Yehuda's Pocket English-Hebrew Hebrew-English Dictionary* (New York: Pocket Books, 1991).

We must remember that Ben Clifford wrote this little twenty-five page essay simply to help beginning students remember how to recognize and correctly draw each Hebrew letter. I believe he succeeded admirably in doing this. Several of his descriptions evoke bizarre and unforgettable images: "Tau looks like a Resh holding a dead dolphin by the tail," or "Lamed looks like a snake that has swallowed a brick and is now having second thoughts."

As a purely Qabalistic work, however, this essay is far from comprehensive. His comments on the letters are limited primarily to basic definitions of the letters. Occasionally he muses briefly about how the primitive meanings may be applied to cosmic, psychological, or sexual principles, but for the most part, he seems satisfied to offer us simply an appetizer to further food for thought.

The stunning exception is found in his comments on the letter Yod. I strongly urge the reader to carefully read and re-read that section. In 210 words, Ben Clifford casually reveals the supreme symbolic secret of creation by drawing our attention to that most mysterious of natural numbers known to mathematicians as the Greek letter Phi, and to architects as the Golden Mean or Golden Section. This number, or ratio (1.6180339887499), like the irrational

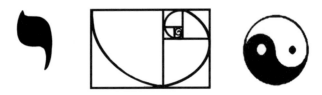

Figure 6. Yod, the Golden Mean, Yin-Yang.

number Pi, seems to issue from, and set the pattern for, the basic structure of the entire cosmos. But, unlike other abstract numbers, the pattern set by Phi is revealed naturally and universally in all living things and all things that grow and develop in stages. One of the most striking examples of this pattern of growth can found in the shell of the nautilus, which, when cross-sectioned, reveals a breathtaking repeating pattern of what looks like extended Hebrew Yods or English letter Gs. On a grander scale, it can be found in the formation of the great spiral nebulae. This primal pattern of patterns is, indeed, the "G" signature of the "Great Architect of the Universe," the name by which Freemasons refer to Deity. As far as I know, Ben Clifford is the first Qabalist (or alleged Qabalist) to make this profound and fundamental connection.

I suppose inevitably there will be those who view as crude and offensive Ben Clifford's sexual allusions to Hebrew letters and other elements of Qabalistic study. Admittedly, at first glance it does appear that he places an inordinate emphasis on phalluses and vaginas, wombs and sperm, and such. As he is no longer here to defend himself, I feel I must say a few words on the Rabbi's behalf.

For the last two thousand years there has been a concerted effort by those who would guide the spiritual life of Western Civilization, to divorce human life from nature (on one end of the scale) and from God on the other. We are taught that we are superior to other living things because *we* were created in the image of the Deity and can do what we damn well please with the environment and the creatures around us. At the same time, we are told that the Deity is outside of us—that we stand eternally *separated* from It because of an ambiguous act of disobedience committed by our mythological ancestors— that we are cursed by the simple act of being born. Ben Clifford's 7th, 8th, and 9th Command-Rants cleanly expose this spiritual schizophrenia as a cruel and unwholesome fraud.

Everything in Heaven and Earth is connected to everything in Heaven and Earth.

Everything in Heaven and Earth is the reflection of everything in Heaven and Earth.

Everything in Heaven and Earth contains the pattern of everything in Heaven and Earth.

Nothing can be separated from anything else, including all aspects of the human condition. To discuss sexual matters within a religious context is as proper as discussing matters of scripture, or mathematics, or physics. Since a great deal of our time is already spent thinking about sex, it is only logical that a significant part of our meditations on any subject should be dominated by the universal truths inherent in sexual imagery. Ben Clifford was fond of misquoting Freud and often told his students, "Sometimes a cigar is just a cigar… and sometimes it is the supreme creative force of the universe."

I applaud Ben Clifford's healthy attitude and casual candor. Furthermore, I can say with some small measure of authority that much of what he has to say in this area reveals the most profound level of understanding. I advise the serious student to ponder his words carefully. To those who are still offended or embarrassed by the Rabbi's comments I say, "Thank you for buying this book—now grow up!"

Meet the Hebrew Alphabet

A Brief Introduction to the Letters of the Hebrew Alphabet—
Their Formation, Meanings, and Correspondences

By

Rabbi Lamed Ben Clifford

Does God speak Hebrew?

Hell no! God's a Chicken Qabalist and doesn't worry about it. Do you actually think there is a white-bearded giant in the clouds who created the universe and everything in it by belching out nouns and verbs right out of some celestial edition of Ben-Yehuda's Hebrew dictionary? I don't think so. The creative fiat, the language of the Deity, is not one of grunts and gurgles and hisses and sighs. It is a language of numbers. Numbers do all the work. What distinguishes the Hebrew alphabet is not its pronunciation or its words and grammar, but its intimate relationship with numbers.

If God "said" anything in the beginning, it was most likely, "Let there be 3." That's all that needed to be said because, as we learned in the Sepher Yetzirah, the 3 dimensions then just took off on their own and extended from the central point to instantly form 7 and 12 spatial coordinates—a tight little 22-piece toolbox of creation.

Let's start our brief study of the Hebrew alphabet by first observing that the 22 letters are divided into 3 categories: 3 Mother letters, 7 Double letters, and 12 Simple letters. 3—7—12. What a coincidence.

3 MOTHER LETTERS

[representing three primal elements]

א Aleph	מ Mem	ש Shin
⊕	▽	△
Air	Water	Fire

7 DOUBLE LETTERS

[representing the seven planets of the ancients]

ב Beth	ד Daleth	כ Kaph	פ Peh	ג Gimel	ר Resh	ת Tau
☿	♀	♃	♂	☽	☉	♄
Mercury	Venus	Jupiter	Mars	Moon	Sun	Saturn

12 SIMPLE LETTERS

[representing the twelve signs of the zodiac]

ה Heh	♈ Aries	ל Lamed	♎ Libra
ו Vau	♉ Taurus	נ Nun	♏ Scorpio
ז Zain	♊ Gemini	ס Samekh	♐ Sagittarius
ח Cheth	♋ Cancer	ע Ayin	♑ Capricorn
ט Teth	♌ Leo	צ Tzaddi	♒ Aquarius
י Yod	♍ Virgo	ק Qoph	♓ Pisces

*Figure 7. These 22 Letters join the 10 Sephiroth
and, in doing so, create the Tree of Life.*

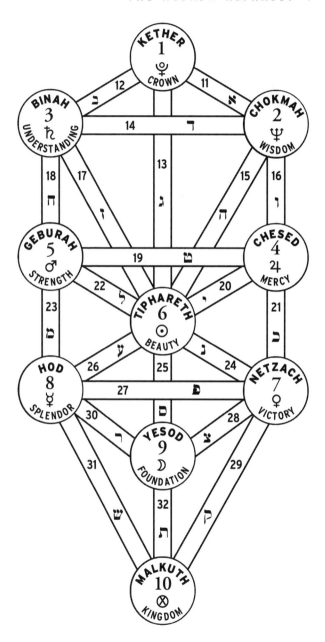

Figure 8. The Tree of Life.

1

א

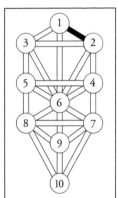

Aleph—A

Aleph is Path No. 11. It joins Kether (Crown) to Chokmah (Wisdom).

Aleph doesn't look like any other Hebrew letter and is therefore easy to recognize. It has one long diagonal bar that looks like a banana separating two small Yods. The Yod at the top right is connected to the banana at midpoint by a thin line (a Yod on a stick). The Yod at the bottom left is flattened at the bottom like a foot and is connected to the banana underneath its left shoulder.

Aleph is spelled אלף (ALP). The three letters enumerate to 111 (or using Peh Final 831) and mean "ox." In ancient cultures, the ox that pulled the furrowing plough was a supreme symbol of the fertilizing force of creation. Aleph is a letter of breath and the closest thing the Hebrew alphabet has to a vowel. As the plough of the ox penetrates and aerates the soil, so the breath of life penetrates and vivifies you and me. Oh hell! I'll come out and say it—the Air of Aleph is more than just the firmament of atmosphere surrounding Earth—it is the Life-Force itself, the Prana of the Hindus, the active ingredient that makes the Holy Spirit holy). Give it some respect!

Aleph is one of the 3 Mother Letters and represents the element Air.

TAROT TRUMP: The Fool.

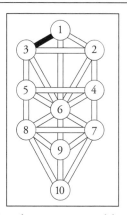

2

Beth—B

Beth is Path No. 12. It joins Kether (Crown) to Binah (Understanding).

Note that the roof of Beth is an elongated Yod that slides to the right and drips down to smoothly form a leg. The leg is connected to a long right-leaning parallelogram that serves as the base of the letter. The leg connects *near* but not *at* the right edge of the base.

Beth **ב** Do not confuse with Kaph **כ**

Beth is spelled **בית** (BYTh). The three letters enumerate to 412 and mean "house." Its shape suggests a cave, the earliest house. In biblical times, a house was often a tent. A house is fundamentally a container, but it is also a shelter, a sanctuary, and a resting place, and most importantly, a place to exist. Beth is the fundamental structure of the universe, a container of existence, a receptacle of life, an atom, a living cell, a body. Astrologers divide the Heavens into twelve "houses." Family bloodlines and households are also considered "houses," such as the House of David or the House of Frankenstein.

Beth is one of the 7 Double Letters and represents the planet Mercury.

TAROT TRUMP: The Magician.

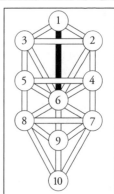

Gimel—G

Gimel is Path No. 13. It joins Kether (Crown) to Tiphareth (Beauty).

Gimel starts with a Yod that extends straight down from its bottom tear. This leg connects to a short right-leaning parallelogram that serves as the base of the letter. Note that the leg connects only partially to the top right edge of the base:

ג Do not confuse with Nun נ

Gimel is spelled גמל (GML). The three letters enumerate to 73 and mean "camel," also *to couple* or *team up*. Like the ox, a camel is an animal domesticated to the service of humanity. The ox, however, is exploited in the cause of nourishment, the camel in the cause of communication. A camel is the "ship of the desert," a vehicle of life and commerce, capable of crossing the vast abyss of sand. The Path of Gimel on the Tree of Life also crosses the Abyss and joins Kether to Tiphareth.

In Aramaic (the language allegedly spoken by Jesus) the word *camel* and the word *rope* are spelled exactly the same, "gamla." I wasn't there, so I can't say for sure, but I'll bet in Matthew 19:24 Jesus says, "It is easier for a *rope* (not *camel*) to go through the eye of a needle, than for a rich man to enter into the kingdom of God." Duh!

Gimel is one of the 7 Double Letters and represents the Moon.

TAROT TRUMP: The High Priestess.

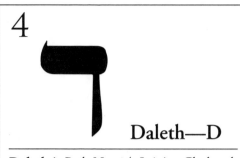

Daleth—D

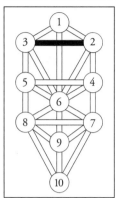

Daleth is Path No. 14. It joins Chokmah (Wisdom) to Binah (Understanding).

Daleth has a firm level roof. It is connected by a leg on the right side. Note that the leg connects *near* but not at the right edge of the roof. A little part of the roof hangs over the leg.

ד Do not confuse with Resh ר

Daleth is spelled דלת (DLTh). The three letters enumerate to 434 and mean "door." A door is a valve that can bar or accommodate both the entrance and exit of things. It is a tent flap, a threshold, and a gate. Walk out of the door of your house and you move from the unity of your home to the multiplicity of the world and vice versa.

The most important "door" for humans is a woman's womb and/or vagina. It accommodates the entrance of the fertilizing male member, and nine months later, it is the door through which we all enter the world.

Daleth is one of the 7 Double Letters and represents the planet Venus.

TAROT TRUMP: The Empress.

5

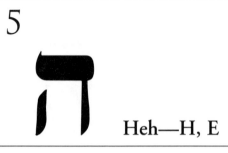

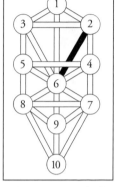

Heh—H, E

Heh is Path No. 15. It joins Chokmah (Wisdom) to Tiphareth (Beauty).

Heh is drawn exactly like Daleth, but has an additional left leg. Note that the left leg does not touch the roof.

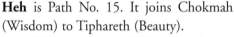 Do not confuse with Cheth ‌ or Tau ‌

Heh is spelled ‌‌ (HH). The two letters enumerate to 10 and mean "window." Also *to breathe, to exist, to become,* and *to desire.* A window is a transparent door, an eye through which we look out on the world. From within the house, we look out of the window at approaching visitors, so we can decide who to allow through the door and who to bar. A window also allows light and air to penetrate the house. Heh also means the *identification of a star,* as for navigation or astrology.

Its shape introduces the concept of openings—a small opening on the left and a large opening from below. This is suggestive of all things receptive, female, or negatively charged.

Heh is one of the 12 Simple Letters and represents the zodiacal sign of Aries.

TAROT TRUMP: The Emperor.

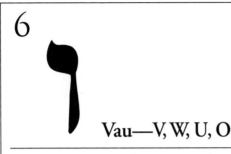

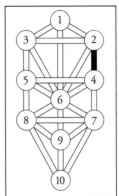

6

Vau—V, W, U, O

Vau is Path No. 16. It joins Chokmah (Wisdom) to Chesed (Mercy).

Vau starts with a Yod at the top that extends straight down from its bottom tear to form a right leg. Note that the leg connects to the top right edge of the Yod.

ℸ Do not confuse with Zain ℸ

Vau is spelled וו (VV). The two letters enumerate to 12 and mean "nail" or "hook" or "pin." A hook can be used to suspend things from above. Nails and pins are sharp, pointy things that join two objects together by means of penetration. By its very shape, it represents the phallus. This implies union (yoga), and union with God is the goal of all mystics, especially Chicken Qabalists. The process is theoretically simple. Find the proper Vau and you can nail yourself to God! This concept of union is further underscored when we remember the letter Vau is the Hebrew conjunction "and."

Its shape introduces the concept of penetration, and is suggestive of all things aggressive, male, or positively charged.

Vau is a one of the 12 Simple Letters and represents the zodiacal sign of Taurus.

TAROT TRUMP: The Hierophant

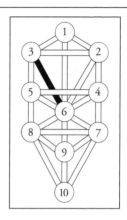

7

Zain—Z

Zain is Path No. 17. It joins Binah (Understanding) to Tiphareth (Beauty).

Zain is a Yod with a leg dropping down from its bottom center.

ק Do not confuse with Vau ו

Zain is spelled זין (ZYN). The three letters enumerate to 67 (or using Nun Final 717) and mean "sword." A sword is a weapon of both offense and defense. It is the weapon of invoked force. It can be brandished as a deterrent or wielded to enforce the decisions of authority. A sword is also an instrument of division, separating one thing from another (like your enemy's head from his shoulders), and of discretion and analysis, separating one idea from another. In a way, it is just the opposite of Vau, which unites things.

Zain is one of the 12 Simple Letters and represents the zodiacal sign of Gemini.

TAROT TRUMP: The Lovers.

8

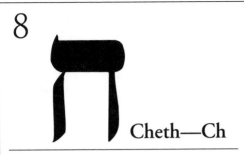

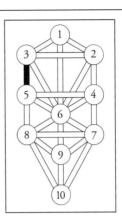

Cheth—Ch

Cheth is Path No. 18. It joins Binah (Understanding) to Geburah (Strength).

Cheth is drawn exactly like Heh but both legs touch the roof.

ח Do not confuse with Heh ה or Tau ת

Cheth is spelled חית (ChYTh). The three letters enumerate to 418 and mean "field" and "fence." A fenced-in field implies culti-vated land—land that has been set apart, defined, and then plowed by the *ox*. A fence encloses an area and sets it apart from the surrounding area. It is a *wall*, a *hedge*, a *membrane*, a *shell*, a *womb*, a *crust*, a *fortress*, a *citadel*. It surrounds and protects the sacred life and light within from the danger and darkness without. Cheth also indicates the Life-Force itself, and anything living.

Cheth is one of the 12 Simple Letters and represents the zodi-acal sign of Cancer.

TAROT TRUMP: The Chariot.

9

Teth—T

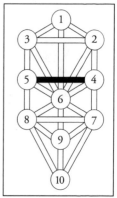

Teth is Path No. 19. It joins Chesed (Mercy) to Geburah (Strength).

Teth has a firm rectangular base from which sprout a mini-Zain from the left edge and a sharp leftward-crashing wave arising from the right edge. I think it looks like the profile of a duck swimming on the water looking back at a big Yod that's stuck to the tip of its tail. Note that the duck's bill does not touch the Yod on its tail.

ט Do not confuse with Mem מ

Teth is spelled טית (TYTh). The three letters enumerate to 419 and mean "serpent." Human beings are vertebrates and our spines are home to unimaginable energy and power. We are snakes with arms and legs, and this serpent energy is the key to our divine birthright. Like a snake swallowing its tail, there is truly no end to the mystery of the serpent. The one that tempted Eve is the same one that Moses elevated on a pole, and the same one that Jesus told us to be as "wise as."

It is also interesting to note that the ancients were aware that individual sperm cells look like tiny snakes with giant (lion-like) heads.

Teth is one of the 12 Simple Letters and represents the zodiacal sign of Leo.

TAROT TRUMP: Strength.

10

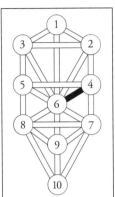

Yod—Y, I, J

Yod is Path No. 20. It joins Chesed (Mercy) to Tiphareth (Beauty).

Yod is a flame. Blow upon it and you create all the other letters of the alphabet. Yod is my favorite Hebrew letter because it is so simple. It is the perfect pattern of primal creation—a point extending to become the whirling motion. It is Phi, the seed of the Golden Spiral; the mystic "G" in your grandfather's Masonic ring; the Yin and Yang; the human embryo; the blueprint of the ram's horn and the nautilus; the swirling cream in your coffee, and the billowing dynamics of smoke and air and water. It sets the pattern for our fingerprints, our DNA and the shape of great galaxies. It is the primal male-Shiva divine fire that plunges joyously into the female-Shakti ocean of divine water.

Yod is spelled יוד (YVD) [which is not a public health question]. The three letters enumerate to 20 and mean "hand." Using Qabalistic logic, *Yod* is the key creative instrument of the Deity in the same way that the *hand* is a key creative instrument of human beings. Follow me? The human hand, however, is only the mundane member of creation. A secret and more profound equivalent of the creative hand is the spermatozoon, itself, of which I believe Yod is the most appropriate hieroglyph.

Yod is one of the 12 Simple Letters and represents the zodiacal sign of Virgo.

TAROT TRUMP: The Hermit.

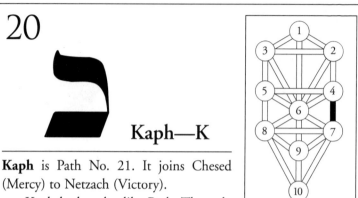

20

Kaph—K

Kaph is Path No. 21. It joins Chesed (Mercy) to Netzach (Victory).

Kaph looks a lot like Beth. The only difference is Kaph's leg connects at the far right edge of the base.

ב Do not confuse with Beth ב

ך Kaph Final

Kaph is also one of five Hebrew letters that has a different shape and numerical value when it appears as the final letter of a word. The five Final Letters are longer or wider than regular letters. Kaph (Final) looks like Daleth with a shorter roof and a long leg. The numerical value of Kaph Final is 500.

Kaph is spelled ךכ (KP). The three letters enumerate to 100 (or using Peh Final 820) and mean "palm." Kaph even looks like the profile of a hand opening to grasp something, the thumb forming the base (the hand of Yod in the process of creation). At the risk of sounding crude, we must remember that for young men, the palm of the hand was our first sexual partner. Palmists are quick to point out that our destiny can be read in the palms of our hands. Kaph's association with Jupiter (the Tarot's Wheel of Fortune) would underscore this association.

Kaph is one of the 7 Double Letters and represents the planet Jupiter.

TAROT TRUMP: The Wheel of Fortune.

30

ל

Lamed—L

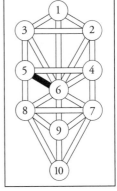

Lamed is Path No. 22. It joins Geburah (Strength) to Tiphareth (Beauty).

Lamed. The little Yod at the top of Lamed towers over and above the other letters and makes it easy to recognize. Lamed looks like a snake that has swallowed a brick and is now having second thoughts.

Lamed is spelled למד (LMD). The three letters enumerate to 74 and mean "ox goad," also *to teach* and *to discipline*. The ox goad is the pointy stick that prods the ox (א—Aleph) down the straight and narrow furrows of the field. Without the ox goad, the ox would be an undomesticated animal (and Aleph would spin completely out of control). This indicates that there is a special relationship between Lamed and Aleph. אל (AL) is the name of God most holy and לא (LA) means "not." Lamed makes sure that the infinite power of the Holy Spirit of Aleph is channeled into what we perceive as natural patterns.

I am proud to have been named Lamed because it also means *teacher* and *scholar*.

Lamed is one of the 12 Simple Letters and represents the zodiacal sign of Libra.

Tarot trump: Justice

40

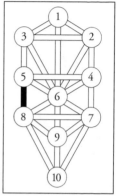

Mem—M

Mem is Path No. 23. It joins Geburah (Strength) to Hod (Splendor).

Mem, as we recall, looks a lot like Teth. There are three differences: (1) Mem's base is a parallelogram; (2) The left leg does not touch the base; (3) The leftward-crashing wave touches the upper left Yod.

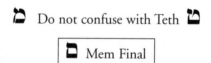

If we are still looking at a duck swimming on the water, the duck has reached back with its bill and has pulled its tail completely off.

Mem is the second Final Letter. When used at the end of a word, it looks like an elongated Samekh with a squared base. The numerical value of Mem Final is 600.

Mem is spelled **מים** (MYM). The three letters enumerate to 90 (or using Mem Final 650) and mean "water." It also suggests all things liquid, especially life-giving or life-supporting fluids, such as blood, or semen, or wine.

Mem is one of the 3 Mother Letters and represents the element Water.

TAROT TRUMP: The Hanged Man.

50

Nun—N

Nun is Path No. 24. It joins Tiphareth (Beauty) to Netzach (Victory).

Nun looks a lot like Gimel. The only difference is Nun's leg connects solidly with the base.

ב Do not confuse with Gimel ג

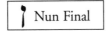

Nun is the third Final letter. When used at the end of a word, it looks like a Vau with a very long leg. It also looks like that little mirror on a stick that the dentist sticks in your mouth. The numerical value of Nun Final is 700.

Nun is spelled נון (NVN). The three letters enumerate to 106 (or using Nun Final 756) and mean "fish." Fish are known for their ability to breed like crazy. Nun represents fecundity and regeneration. When dead, fish decay rapidly and smell terrible. Nun is also the letter of decay. This really isn't a paradox when you consider the fact that fertilizer smells terrible, but helps things grow.

Nun is one of the 12 Simple Letters and represents the zodiacal sign of Scorpio.

TAROT TRUMP: Death.

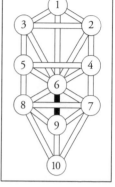

60

Samekh—S

Samekh is Path No. 25. It joins Tiphareth (Beauty) to Yesod (Foundation).

Samekh has a roof and right leg identical with Heh and Cheth. The right leg connects with the top edge of a broad parallelogram. A left leg reaches from the left edge of the base to the left underside of the roof.

ם Do not confuse with Mem (Final) ם

Samekh is spelled סמך (SMK). The three letters enumerate to 120 (or using Kaph Final 600) and mean "tent peg" or "prop." In biblical times, the tent peg was a most important and potent symbol because it was an absolutely indispensable tool for the proper erection of the tent. Not only did it ensure the tent would rise toward Heaven, but it also and simultaneously secured it to Earth.

All this pointy phallic symbolism seems rather paradoxical when we consider the extremely female shape of the letter itself. Samekh's meaning is phallic, but its shape suggests all things circular; the canopy of Heaven, the vagina, the womb.

Samekh is one of the 12 Simple Letters and represents the zodiacal sign of Sagittarius.

TAROT TRUMP: Temperance.

70

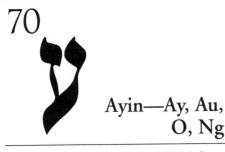

Ayin—Ay, Au, O, Ng

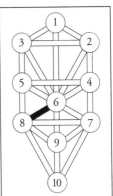

Ayin is Path No. 26. It joins Tiphareth (Beauty) to Hod (Splendor).

Ayin is very distinctive. It is built upon a bold right-leaning diagonal banana. There is one Yod connected to the top of the banana, and a Zain stabs the banana's top mid-section. It looks very much like an English lower case "y."

Do not confuse with Tzaddi (Final)

Ayin is spelled עין (AYN). The three letters enumerate to 130 (or using Nun Final 780) and mean "eye." Unlike a window (Heh) that allows light and images to both enter and exit the house, the eye is more of a one-way proposition. Through the eye our inward being looks out at the world. For this reason (and numerous others) Ayin has traditionally been associated with the *meatus,* the opening at the tip of the penis, through which the semen passes on its one-way adventure to eggland. Ayin also means fountain, spring, source. Do I need to draw us a picture here?

Ayin is one of the 12 Simple Letters and represents the zodiacal sign of Capricorn.

TAROT TRUMP: The Devil.

80

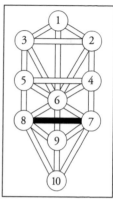

Peh—P, Ph, F

Peh is Path No. 27. It joins Netzach (Victory) to Hod (Splendor).

Peh is exactly like Kaph, only it sports a distinctive tongue that dangles from the roof of its mouth.

Peh is the fourth Final letter. When used at the end of a word it looks like a long Vau with a tongue. The numerical value of Peh Final is 800.

Peh is spelled פה (PH). The two letters enumerate to 85 and mean "mouth." What goes in the mouth as *nourishment* is vital to human life, but what comes out of the mouth as *speech* is vital to our minds. It is no coincidence that the first and most important gift the mythological gods gave to humans was the gift of speech. Speech is one of the primary characteristics that separate humans from other living creatures. Once we started talking, our thought patterns were drastically overhauled. This had a profound effect upon our ancestors' self-image and view of reality, not to mention the way our brains would evolve from that point onward.

Peh is one of the 7 Double Letters and represents the planet Mars.

TAROT TRUMP: The Tower.

90

Tzaddi—Tz, X

Tzaddi is Path No. 28. It joins Netzach (Victory) to Yesod (Foundation).

Tzaddi is sometimes confused with Ayin. It looks like a man with a huge pompadour haircut kneeling forward. He has just been stabbed in the back with a Yod on a stick.

 Tzaddi Final

Tzaddi is the fifth Final letter. When used at the end of a word it looks like a regular Tzaddi that got up off its knees. The numerical value of Tzaddi Final is 900.

Tzaddi is spelled צדי (TzDY). The three letters enumerate to 104 and mean "fish-hook." It also relates to words such as *hunt, hunter, hunted, to lie in wait, capture,* and *adversary.*

Tzaddi is one of the 12 Simple Letters and represents the zodiacal sign of Aquarius.

TAROT TRUMP: The Star.

100

ק

Qoph—Q

Qoph is Path No. 29. It joins Netzach (Victory) to Malkuth (Kingdom).

Qoph is quite unique. It is very similar to an English capital P with none of its components touching. It also looks like a left-facing profile of Elvis Presley with really long eyebrows drooping down past his chin.

Qoph is spelled קוף (QVP). The three letters enumerate to 186 (or using Peh Final 906) and means "back of head." Qoph really must be meditated upon in conjunction with the following letter Resh, which means "the face" or "the front of the head." The back of the head is the location of the cerebellum and the medulla oblongata (also known by the Hindus as the "mouth of God"). This area is the most primitive part of our brain, and could care less about the evening news or your job or what wine to drink with fish. It keeps itself active even when we are asleep, unconscious or otherwise wiped out. Qoph is the Hebrew letter of *sleep*. It also has a very strange assortment of other meanings, including *monkey, anus, vomit,* and *eye of a needle.* (Go figure.)

Qoph is one of the 12 Simple Letters and represents the zodiacal sign of Pisces.

TAROT TRUMP: The Moon.

200

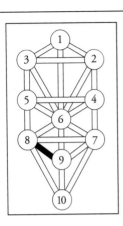

Resh—R

Resh is Path No. 30. It joins Hod (Splendor) to Yesod (Foundation).

Resh has a firm level roof that connects smoothly to a right leg.

ר Do not confuse with Daleth ד

Resh is spelled ריש (RYSh). The three letters enumerate to 510 and mean "head" or "face." Resh is also suggestive of leadership (like the *head* of an organization); or of position (like head of the line); or of quality (like *Supreme* Commander).

It is really only right and relevant that Resh is regarded as the radiant representation of all that is royal and regal. The words *rex, roi, regina, regent, rule* and *reign,* remain as remarkable reminders of Resh's resplendent renown—a reality which rates our respect and reverent remembrance.

Resh is one of the 7 Double Letters and represents the Sun.

TAROT TRUMP: The Sun.

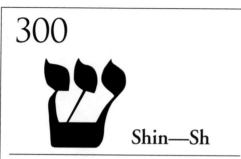

300

Shin—Sh

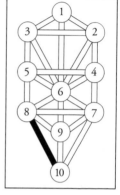

Shin is Path No. 31. It joins Hod (Splendor) to Malkuth (Kingdom).

Shin is perhaps the most beautiful letter in the Hebrew alphabet of flames. It is the glory of three Yods atop a horned crown. The left Yod is a Zain, the right Yod is a waving Vau, and the center Yod—well—the center Yod looks like your basic Yod on a stick.

Shin is spelled שׁין (ShYN). The three letters enumerate to 360 (or using Nun Final 1010) and mean "tooth." Qabalistic tradition holds the letter Shin in particular reverence. If Aleph is the active ingredient of the Holy Spirit, Shin is the Holy Spirit itself. Its number, 360, is also the sum of the letters of the Hebrew words RVCh ALHIM which means the *Breath of God.* When the letter Shin is introduced into the middle of the word יהוה (YHVH) Jehovah, it becomes יהשוה (YHShVH) Jeshuah—Jesus.

Shin is one of the 3 Mother Letters and represents both the element Fire and the element Spirit.

TAROT TRUMP: **Judgement.**

400

Tau—Th, T

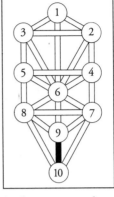

Tau is Path No. 32. It joins Yesod (Foundation) to Malkuth (Kingdom).

Tau is the last letter of the Hebrew alphabet. It is formed just like a Resh, but it is also supported on the left by a slightly curved leg with an incredibly swollen foot. Tau also looks like a Resh holding a dead dolphin by the tail.

ת Do not confuse with Heh ה, Cheth ח or Peh Final ף

Tau is spelled תו (ThV). The two letters enumerate to 406 and mean "mark" or "cross" or "signature." It can mean *to seal, to sign off on* and *to witness*. Aleph and Tau is the Hebrew equivalent of Alpha and Omega. The word אמת (AMT) (made up of the first, middle, and the last letters in the Hebrew alphabet) means "Truth."

Tau is one of the 7 Double Letters and represents both the planet Saturn and the element Earth.

TAROT TRUMP: The World.

Table 1. Hebrew Letters, Attributes, and Correspondences.

Hebrew Letter and English Equivalent		Number Value	Spelling and Number	Meaning	Letter Type	Attribute	Tarot Trump
א	A	1	אלף ALP 111	Ox	Mother	Air	O Fool
ב	B	2	בית BYTh 412	House	Double	Mercury	I Magus
ג	G	3	גמל GML 73	Camel	Double	Moon	II High Priestess
ד	D	4	דלת DLTh 434	Door	Double	Venus	III Empress
ה	H	5	הה HH 10	Window	Simple	Aries	IV Emperor
ו	V,W, U, F, O	6	וו VV 2	Nail	Simple	Taurus	V Hierophant
ז	Z	7	זין ZYN 67	Sword	Simple	Gemini	VI Lovers
ח	Ch	8	חית ChYTh 418	Fence	Simple	Cancer	VII Chariot
ט	T	9	טית TYTh 419	Serpent	Simple	Leo	VIII (or XI) Strength
י	Y, I, J	10	יוד YVD 20	Hand	Simple	Virgo	IX Hermit
כ (ך)	K	20 or 500 (Final)	כף KP 100	Palm of Hand	Double	Jupiter	X Fortune

Table 1. Hebrew Letters, Attributes, and Correspondences (cont.).

Hebrew Letter and English Equivalent		Number Value	Spelling and Number	Meaning	Letter Type	Attribute	Tarot Trump
ל	L	30	למד LMD 74	Ox Goad	Simple	Libra	XI (or VIII) Justice
מ (ם)	M	40 or 600 (Final)	מים MYM 90	Water	Mother	Water	XII Hanged Man
נ (ן)	N	50 or 700 (Final)	נון NVN 106	Fish	Simple	Scorpio	XIII Death
ס	S	60	סמך SMK 120	Prop Hand	Simple	Sagittarius	XIV Temperance
ע	Ay, A'a, O, Ng	70	עין AYN 130	Eye	Simple	Capricorn	XV Devil
פ (ף)	P, Ph, F	80 or 800 (Final)	פה PH 85	Mouth	Double	Mars	XVI Tower
צ (ץ)	Tz	90 or 900 (Final)	צדי TzDI 104	Fish Hook	Simple	Aquarius	XVII Star
ק	Q	100	קוף QVP 186	Back of Head	Simple	Pisces	XVIII Moon
ר	R	200	ריש RISh 510	Head	Double	Sun	XIX Sun
ש	Sh	300	שין ShIN 360	Tooth	Mother	Fire (Spirit)	XX Judgement
ת	T	400	תו ThV 404	Cross, Mark	Double	Saturn (Earth)	XXI Universe

5

THE INEFFABLE NAME OF GOD
AND THE ARK OF THE
COVENANT

Introduced by Lon Milo DuQuette

The Qabalah doesn't enable me to merely interpret what somebody else meant to say, it forces me to hear what I need to hear!
—RABBI LAMED BEN CLIFFORD

As we discovered in Chicken Qabalah FAQs, Rabbi Ben Clifford heaped ridicule upon those who stressed the importance of correct Hebrew pronunciation in Qabalistic study. His sarcasm regarding this subject was never more stinging than in the introduction to his essay on the Tetragrammaton. His fanciful story, in which he purports to explain the true circumstances surrounding the yearly utterance of יהוה by the High Priest of Israel has been justifiably condemned by pious institutions as vulgar and offensive. His reference to the sacred Ark of the Covenant as "Ole Sparky" was particularly insensitive. However, many modern students are tantalized by aspects of his story that raise provocative and intriguing questions, and so, after much deliberation, I have decided to present his essay complete and unedited.

The True Pronunciation of the Ineffable Name of God

An Address by
Rabbi Lamed Ben Clifford
to the 1986 Zerubbabel Institute of Philosophical Youth
Track and Field Team

As I have said on numerous occasions, Hebrew pronunciation is not important to the study of the Qabalah. However, because knowledge of the true pronunciation of the Tetragrammaton יהוה (Yod Heh Vau Heh) has been one of the greatest mysteries in the history of religion, Chicken Qabalists should be aware of the real story behind the correct pronunciation of the Great Name. I will take just a moment at the beginning of today's address to share with you that great secret.

יהוה is called the ineffable name because no one but the High Priest of Israel was allowed to pronounce it, and then only once a year under very peculiar circumstances. For this reason when pious worshippers run across the word in print they substitute the word "Adonai" (Lord) in its place. יהוה first appears in Genesis 2 verse 7:

וייצר יהוה אלהים את האדם עפר מך האדמה ויפח באפיו
נשמה חיים ויהי האדם לנפש חיה.

*And formed YHVH Elohim Adam of the dust of the ground
and breathed into the nostrils the breath (Neshemah) of life
(Chiah) and Adam became a living soul (Nephesh).*

This is commonly translated:
*And the LORD God formed man [of] the dust of the ground,
and breathed into his nostrils the breath of life.*

Up until this verse, the single word **אלהים** (Elohim[1]) was used in Genesis to designate the creator God. In other words, the Deity who created human beings (Adam) by performing CPR on a dirt statue, was a new kind of Elohim, or probably more likely, a specific aspect of Elohim—a *Jehovah*-Elohim.

Why are pious Jews so afraid to pronounce **יהוה** and Christians say the word "Jehovah" with such impunity? The answer is simple. Pious Jews are taught to respect the author or authors of the Pentateuch—mystics who knew that **יהוה** is not really a name at all, but a formula that reveals the basic mechanics of creation and human existence. Christians, on the other hand, historically and by tradition, are encouraged to look no deeper into scripture than the textual narrative, and seem quite satisfied to relegate the magnificent forces of creation to an ill-tempered and fickle mountain-thunder goblin named Jehovah.

Ironically, the Germans gave us the pronunciation Je-ho-vah. It's not a bad try. As we all know, there are no vowels in Hebrew. The little dots and lines (dageshes or points) we see placed over and under the letters of Hebrew words to give clues to pronunciation are a very new innovation to the language. The original texts did not have these points, and so each letter of a word could be pronounced in many different ways.

A simple method to examine just one of the pronunciation choices available is to add a long English vowel sound (A, E, I, O, U) after any given letter. Let's take the letter "B" or Beth **ב** in Hebrew. Beth can sound like "bay," or "bee," or "by," or "bow," or "boo." The

Table 2. Sounding Out the Letters.

' Yod	ה Heh	ו Vau	ה Heh
can be pronounced:	*can be pronounced:*	*can be pronounced:*	*can be pronounced:*
Yah or Jah	Hah or Ah	Vah or Wah	Hah or Ah
Yay or Jay	Hay or Aay	Vay or Way	Hay or Aay
Yeh or Jeh	Heh or Eh	Veh or Weh	Heh or Eh
Yee or Jee or Gee	Hee or Ee	Vee or We	Hee or Ee
Yigh or Jigh or Eye or I	High or Eye or I	Vigh or Why	High or Eye or I
Yoe or Joe	Ho or Oh	Voe or Woe	Ho or Oh
You or Jew	Hoo or Oo or Who	Voo or Woo	Hoo or Oo or Who

letter "P" or Peh פ can sound like "pay," or "pee," or "pie," or "pow," or "poo." If there was a Hebrew word spelled פפ it might be pronounced "pap," or "payp," or "peep," or "pip," or "pipe," or "pop," or "pope," or "pup," or "papa," or "pappy," or "popeye," or "peepee," or "poopoo."[2]

In Table 2 I have itemized just some of the various ways the letters of the Tetragrammaton (Yod, Heh, Vau, Heh) can be sounded out. As you can see, *Jeh-ho-v-ah* is a viable pronunciation of יהוה—

but then—so is *Eye-ah-woo-hoo*. Truly, there is no end to the possible pronunciations of יהוה.

◆ Students of Zen could meditate upon the inscrutable *I-He-We-Who?*

◆ Chanting the mantra *You-Who-Way-High* might bring the devotee to the realization of *I-Who-Way-High?*

◆ Tantric lovers might lure their divine lover by cooing *"Yoo-Hoo! Way-High,"* or at the ecstatic moment they could shout *"Yeh! I-Woo-High?"*

◆ The beauties of paradise might cause vacationing mystics to swoon and utter *"Gee! Ha-Wah-Ee!"*

◆ Perhaps the God of cowboys is called *Gee-Hah! Wah-Hoo!*

Tradition informs us that each year on the tenth day of Tisri (October 10), the Day of Atonement, the High Priest of Israel made three trips into the Most Holy Place of the Great Temple and sprinkled the Ark of the Covenant with blood. Around his leg was tied a long braided rope. The other end of the rope was held by friends of the High Priest who were stationed well outside of the veiled confines of the Most Holy Place. On his third visit to the Most Holy Place, while a multitude of the faithful stood outside the temple and made a lot of noise, the High Priest placed his hands directly upon the Ark and uttered the Ineffable Name as the fiery Deity revealed Itself in cloud and lightning above the lid ("Mercy Seat") of the Ark.

Sounds like a simple ritual, doesn't it? It was not unlike those practiced by Egyptian and Babylonian priests who once or twice a year penetrated their God's sanctum sanctorum, and offered prayers and oblations before sacred statues or other holy objects. What made this ceremony a little different, however, had to do with that rope the High Priest had tied around his leg. It was put there for a very good reason—a reason that, while perhaps not immediately apparent, had everything to do with the correct pronunciation of יהוה.

The rope was needed because every once in a while, at the climax of this supreme ceremony, the High Priest exploded! Not only that, after the poor fellow's spectacular departure, the Holy of Holies filled with so much smoke and fire that it became too dangerous to enter, and the barbecued remains of the Priest had to be dragged from the chamber by the rope.[3] The next year a new High Priest would have to give it another try.

In order for us to understand these strange circumstances and the true pronunciation of the Ineffable Name, it will be necessary for me to talk briefly about the Ark of the Covenant.

First of all, we have to remember that the warring people of Old Testament times were a very superstitious lot. They carried their gods into battle with them in the form of statues, or animals, or other talismanic objects, such as meteorites, or monumental cheeses.[4] If one side happened to win a battle, their god was considered superior to the god of the loosing side. Very often the first thing the vanquished army would do after regrouping was to steal the god of the winners and put it to work for them. We read in First Samuel this happened to the Ark of the Covenant. The Philistines stole it, but later returned it when they discovered it kept killing anyone who tried to move it. Good riddance!

The Ark was a rectangular box that contained the magic goodies from the exodus: Aaron's rod[5] that performed all those miracles in Egypt; a pot of manna, the heavenly food that sprang up like mushrooms in the morning dew and fed the children of the exodus in the wilderness; a pan of liquid referred to as anointing oil, and most importantly, the stone tablets of the Law.

In Exodus chapter 25, יהוה gave very specific directions how the Ark was to be constructed:

And they shall make an ark of shittim wood, two-and-a-half cubits long, and a cubit-and-a-half broad, and a cubit-and-a-half high.[6] And you shall overlay it with pure gold, without and within shall you overlay it, and shall make upon it a crown of gold round about. And you shall cast four rings of gold for it, and put them in the four corners thereof; and two rings on the other side of it. And you shall make poles of shittim wood, and overlay them with gold. And you shall put the poles into the rings by the sides of the ark, that the ark may be borne with them. The poles shall remain in the rings of the ark; they shall never be taken out of them. And you shall put into the ark the testimony which I shall give you. And you shall make a mercy seat[7] of pure gold, two-and-a-half cubits long, and a cubit-and-a-half broad.[8] And you shall make two cherubim of gold, of cast work shall you make them, on the two sides of the mercy seat. And make one cherub on the one side, and the other cherub on the other side of the mercy seat; thus you shall make two cherubim on the two sides thereof. And the cherubim shall spread forth their wings on high, covering the mercy seat with their wings, and their faces shall look one to another; toward the mercy seal shall the faces of the cherubim be. And you shall put the mercy seat on the top of the ark; and in the ark you shall put the testimony that I shall give you. And there I will meet you, and I will commune with you from above the mercy seat, from between the two cherubim which are upon the ark of the testimony, of all things which I will command you concerning the children of Israel.

The Ark was a lethal weapon and the Israelites treated it like one. They kept it wrapped in cloth and leather, and the men who carried it had to wear special clothes and special shoes. That didn't always help. The Bible tells us that people who accidentally touched or got too near the Ark were struck by lightning or consumed by flashes of fire.

The Great Temple of Solomon appears to have been built not so much as a house of worship, but as a prison for the dangerous and unpredictable Ark. The Holy of Holies where the Ark rested was built like a containment chamber, a perfect cube, thirty feet long, thirty feet wide, and thirty feet high. The floor, walls, and ceiling were lined with pure gold, weighing an estimated 45,000 pounds, and riveted in place with golden nails. Sometimes the Ark would belch out so much smoke that the Priests of the Temple were driven completely out of the building and could not perform their routine duties.[9]

It doesn't take a rocket scientist to see that a wooden box with a double lining of gold and closed with a slab of gold, containing pots of mysterious substances, heavy plates and rods submerged in a pan of liquid, was in all likelihood a gigantic and highly unstable battery. The two cherubim on the lid served as the anode and cathode, and a spark or "arc" (the flaming presence of God) jumped madly between the tips of the two highly conductive golden wings.

I can hear you laughing, dear students, but I must remind you that viable batteries have been found in Egyptian tombs of this period and before.[10] I am confident if you review the biblical description of the Ark, and its deadly behavior, you will find nothing inconsistent with the performance of such a primitive electrical device. Such a spectacular and deadly lightshow would most certainly have been an awful spectacle of terror, and a very useful tool if one wanted to keep the troops in line during a 40-year campout.

The High Priest must have been a pretty brave fellow to enter that room and play electrical Russian roulette with "Ole Sparky." As he lay both hands upon that terrible device, his flesh would divert the current that normally arced between the Cherubic wings and for one spectacular moment the power of יהוה literally dwelt in his contorting body. If he survived the event, he was most likely transformed into a very mellow holy man, exhibiting the same docile behavior and mystical inscrutability of patients of modern shock therapy. I would guess he was also pretty interesting to talk to—full of spiritual insights and profound messages from God.

So that, dear ones, is the secret of the Ark of the Covenant. But, I hear you asking, what about the true pronunciation of יהוה the ineffable name of God? Well, I think every year it was pronounced a little differently, but if I were to give you a general idea of how it sounded, I would say it sounded something like . . .

YAAAAAAAAAAHEEEEeeeE

WAAAAAAAOOOooOOOooo

AAAAAAAAAAAAAHAAAA

AAAAAAAAAAAAAAAAA...!

6

THE FOUR
QABALISTIC WORLDS AND
THE FOUR PARTS OF THE SOUL

Introduced by Lon Milo DuQuette

There aren't really four Qabalistic Worlds—only one with amnesia.
—RABBI LAMED BEN CLIFFORD

In the Spring of 1991, Rabbi Ben Clifford became obsessed with the idea of making a Qabalistic documentary. He approached several Southern California filmmakers who predictably gave him no encouragement whatsoever. Undaunted, he began in earnest to write the script. He was absolutely convinced that, *"Once the Qliphotic demons of media see the Assiahic manifestation of my Briahesque genius, they will immediately recognize its pure Atziluthness and transform themselves into angels of Yetzirah and demand to be part of its full materialization in Assiah."*[1]

The documentary, of course, was never made. Although the Rabbi claimed to have finished writing the entire text, no finished manuscript has ever been discovered. The largest and most complete remnant of the script remains in the possession of Dr. I. Z. Gilford, Ben Clifford's veterinarian, who found it lining the floor of the Rabbi's rooftop pigeon coop.

Fortunately, for present and future Chicken Qabalists, this surviving fragment deals with the all-important subjects of the Tetragrammaton (יהוה Yod Heh Vau Heh), the four Qabalistic worlds, and the four parts of the human soul. I think you will agree with me that it is a pity that the documentary was never produced. The Rabbi had a surprisingly keen sense of how familiar visual images can be used to communicate abstract concepts. Dr. Gilford, who has graciously allowed me to reproduce the Rabbi's the manuscript, has requested that I reproduce the material complete with Ben Clifford's somewhat amateurish notes for stage directions, casting, and blocking. I have respected his wishes, and hope the reader will use "the mind's eye" to bring Ben Clifford's dream of a Qabalistic documentary to life.

Let's Learn Chicken Qabalah

AN ESOTERIC DOCUMENTARY WRITTEN AND NARRATED BY

RABBI LAMED BEN CLIFFORD

PART I

The Four Qabalistic Worlds
Sketch: The Qabalistic Elevator

SCENE I

Location: Parking lot of a four-story office building.

RABBI:

This building is the universe. Not only the physical universe which we perceive with its awkward limitations of time and space—but the whole ball of wax—the totality of every dimension, energy, and aspect of consciousness. Qabalists tell us that each of us is a miniature version of this totality.

[pointing to building]

All that was, is, and shall be is right in there...

[pointing to his own heart]

...and right here.

This Supreme One is too profoundly simple for our poor minds to contemplate. In order for us to even begin to speculate upon the nature of this One we are forced to hypothetically divide it up and consider it in various parts.

If we divide it into two parts we can consider it in terms of dualities: darkness-light, male-female, on-off, hot-cold; you get the picture.

If we divide it into three parts, we can consider it in terms of the thesis-antithesis-synthesis trinity of your choice; creation-preservation-destruction; father-mother-child; too hot-too cold-just right.

Do you see where this is taking us? The more we divide the Great One, the more knowledge and understanding we uncover from the individual parts. But, at the same time, we drift farther from the abstract perfection of the One.

The ancient Qabalists delighted in dividing the One in many ways, but the primary, and some say, supreme division was by four, and they gave this fourfold Deity a four-letter name: Yod Heh Vau Heh.

[pointing again to building]

That building over there is one building with four floors. Let's go inside and see what One looks like when it is divided into four parts.

RABBI *enters door marked*:

Floor 1

ה

Heh

Assiah

• • •

SCENE II

Location: Furniture warehouse showroom.

[The first interior shot is of a furniture warehouse showroom of chairs. Thousands of chairs of every size and description, even benches, stools, and pews. Rabbi walks over to a huge overstuffed chair, sits down and says:]

RABBI:

Ah . . . . This is what I need. We are in the chair division of the material universe. There are lots of other divisions, too. In fact, there is a section on this floor for absolutely everything in the phenomenal universe, including you and me— a table section, a tree section, a canned soup section, a section for small vibrating appliances—even a section for solar systems and galaxies— all right here on Floor One.

Qabalists call this world Assiah,[2] the material plane. It's the lowest of the four Qabalistic worlds, and is represented by the final letter Heh in the Great Name.

But back to these chairs. Where do they all come from? You might answer that the wood comes from trees, and the nails come from raw metal, and the wool coverings come from sheep, but you would be wrong, because all you are really saying is that the wood comes from the tree section of this floor, the nails from the metal section, and the wool from sheep division of the material plane.

That being the case, where on Earth *do* all these chairs come from? The fact is, nothing on this floor comes from Earth at all. These chairs and everything else in the phenomenal universe only manifest here.

[Rabbi struggles to get out of the easy chair...perhaps has to be helped up by crew member. Once up, he walks toward the elevator. Camera follows.]

To begin to understand where things really come from we have to go one floor up.

RABBI *enters elevator.*

• • •

SCENE III

Location: Interior of elevator.
[From inside the elevator Rabbi pushes button marked:]

• • •

SCENE IV

Location: Blueprint room.

[Elevator door opens to reveal a room where hundreds of blueprints are hung by invisible wires. The room is filled with people in white, short-sleeved shirts, loud ties, and black slacks. All have pocket protectors and wear dark-rimmed glasses (some broken and taped at the bridge). Many are holding pencils, pens, T-squares, compasses, protractors, and other mechanical drawing instruments. They are all engaged in animated conversations, making broad gestures with their hands as they talk.]

RABBI *[voice hushed]:*
    These nerds are angels . . .

[Rabbi is interrupted for a moment by juvenile squeals and wildly irritating laughter from one of the nerds.]

. . . quite low on the hierarchical scale, actually, but they are hard workers and smart as whips.

We are one floor up and directly above the chair area of Assiah, the world of Heh Final. This place is Yetzirah, the world of Vau. It's called the Formative World, and these angels are hard at work putting the final touches on the blueprints for all those chairs down on the first floor. They can't actually make the chairs up here because this is the world of thought, not matter.

[Camera pans to a group of nerds gathered around a slide projector projecting the photo of a chair on a screen. Excited applause and more irritating laughter.]

This level of creation is "the mind's eye." Absolutely everything, tangible or intangible, that is conceived of in the mind, is formed here in Yetzirah.

Artists who know what their paintings should look like before they start painting, composers who can hear their own music in their minds before it is played, grandmas who know in July what the Thanksgiving table should look like, are all communicating directly with the angels on this floor.

But, smart as they are, these guys need inspiration and direction from a higher consciousness. They must take their orders from somewhere else.

RABBI *enters elevator.*

• • •

SCENE V

Location: Interior of elevator.

[From inside the elevator Rabbi pushes button marked:]

Floor 3

ה

Heh

Briah

• • •

SCENE VI

Location: Shower stall of Thomas Edison's bathroom.

[Room is very steamy. Subtitle appears on the screen: "Thomas Edison's bathroom—1877." We hear the sound of running water and the voice of Thomas Edison singing "You Light Up My Life."]

RABBI *[voice hushed]*:

The person in the shower isn't really Thomas Edison. Actually, he's an angel, a very high angel, really. For our purpose, we can even call him an archangel. The reason we find him in the likeness of Edison and taking a nice shower in the great inventor's bathroom is to help us illustrate something about this Qabalistic World—the world of Briah, the Creative World.

Now, Edison didn't invent the chair, but he did invent (or improve upon) an unbelievable number of things that brought revolutionary change to the world; the light bulb, the phonograph, and motion pictures, to name a few. There's no doubt about it, the man was a genius. But we might ask, how could one man possibly invent all of those things? Where did he get the time? Let's watch for a few moments.

[Suddenly the singing stops. The water is turned off. Silence. Then Edison shouts:]

EDISON:

Yesssssssss!

[Edison opens the door to the shower stall and steps out in a cloud of steam. He dances excitedly, naked before the large steamed-over mirror in front of the sink.]

EDISON:

Yes! Yes, Yes, they'll love it! They'll absolutely love it! We'll make millions! Millions! Mary! Mary! Send for Clifford, my chief engineer. Get him in here right now!

RABBI *[voice hushed]*:

Actually, we don't know if Clifford was the name of Edison's chief engineer. For our purposes it doesn't really matter, so I named him after my father.

[Edison's chief engineer timidly enters the bathroom. He is wearing the exact same outfit as the nerd angels in Yetzirah. Edison goes to the steamed-over mirror and begins to draw things on the mirror with his finger.]

EDISON:

Clifford, I've invented a machine that can record and play back sounds—voices—music—body noises—anything!

[Edison outlines a crude cylinder on the mirror—his finger makes a squeaking sound as it rubs the glass.]

EDISON:

Hear that? You know how things make a sound when you rub them together or scratch them? Well, we make a "rubby-scratchy thing" out of a rotating cylinder or something, see? And then you connect it to something else—I don't know what—a something that we then somehow hook up to that telephone diaphragm we made. See? And then somehow you get the rubby-vibrations to scratch up the "rubby-scratchy thing." Then all we have to do is figure out how to rub those scratches with something else, then maybe run the scratchy vibrations along to another diaphragm or something, so we can replay the same kind of noise that made the scratches on "rubby-scratchy thing" in the first place. See?

[Clifford scratches his head.]

EDISON:

Then, then—You'll love this!

[Edison draws a large cone on the mirror.]

EDISON:

Then you get the scratchy sounds to go in the small end of this cone, see? And when it comes out the big end it's real loud! Real loud! See?

RABBI *[voice hushed]*:

Let's just take a look at that mirror. All we see is a crude cylinder, two squiggly lines, something that looks like a box, and a cone resting on its side with an arrow pointing at the large end and the words, "Big noise comes out here!"

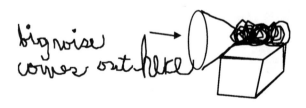

[Clifford stares blankly at the mirror.]

EDISON:

I call it the phonograph. Run along now, and tidy up the details. I want to see a working model by the weekend. I'm going fishing with Hank Ford and Wilbur Wright. There's a good fellow.

RABBI:

Now, I'm not sure that's exactly what happened when the phonograph was invented, but generally speaking, this is just how Edison operated. Very often he would come up with the very vaguest of ideas, scribble down a crude drawing and a few notes, and then turn it over to a team of well-paid and highly motivated assistants. These "angels" would then bring Edison's concept to life by painstakingly inventing all the little devices that would make Edison's inspired big machine work.

Edison's ideas (archangelic inspirations) came from the creative world of Briah, his assistants (angelic executors of the archangelic will) were the workers in the formative world of Yetzirah, who eventually manifested the inventions on the material plane of Assiah.

Or, more simply—Everything in the Material World exists as a pattern in the Formative World that has its motivation for being in the Creative World.

But what is above that?—in the highest Qabalistic world. Atziluth, the World of Yod.

• • •

SCENE VII

Location: Interior of elevator.

[From inside the elevator Rabbi pushes button marked:]

. . .

SCENE VIII

Location: Cloud-filled formless world of swirling light and mists.

[Rabbi stays inside the elevator and holds the door open as camera enters the mist. Ambient music is playing. Within the music we hear the faint sounds of a man and a woman—in unison—making sensuous love sighs. The light pulsates erotically against the undulating clouds giving the abstract appearance of a man and a woman locked in a writhing embrace:]

RABBI *[voice hushed]*:

This is Atziluth, the Archetypal World. Atziluth could be considered the will of the Deity in its purest aspect. It's the highest and most perfect of the four worlds. In Atziluth there is no separation of the male and female aspects of the Deity; they are eternally united in bliss

The remaining three worlds are the products of this ecstatic union, and as we have seen, continue to diminish in purity as we descend to the lower floors.

But, luckily for us, what looks like degenerating energy from the Deity's point of view, looks like creation itself to us pitiful creatures rooting around down on the first floor.

RABBI *[whispering]*:

Remember, we are standing four floors directly above that lovely lounge chair in the chair section of the first floor. Let's see what the Deity has on Its mind.

[Music lowers and the voices can be heard clearly. Voices never speak separately, but always say their lines in perfect unison.]

THE DEITY:

[male and female aspects locked in ecstatic embrace]

"Aaaaah! Was it good for us?

Ooo yes! It's always and eternally good for us.

Mmmm! But we're a bit tired now, aren't we?

Wouldn't we like to rest now?

Oh yes! Yes! Oh, for a moment to pause.

Even ecstasy is boring if it never stops."

RABBI *[whispering]*:

Well, things are pretty vaporous in Archetypal World. Up here in Atziluth there are no forms or images, just pure conscious energy—a dynamo of bliss. But it sounds like even this dynamo needs to kick back and relax on occasion, if only to experience within itself the pulse of an expanding and contracting creation cycle.

Of course, in other sections of this floor, the Deity is germinating other nebulous desires that will eventually manifest on the first floor in Assiah as absolutely everything in the phenomenal universe. But right here in Atziluth, three levels above the chairs in the Material World, the vague desire for rest is unique to this particular section of the Deity's consciousness.

Oh listen! I think a divine impulse from the Atziluthic Deity is about to inspire the Thomas Edison Archangel of chairs one floor down in Briah . . .

[Voices rise in an ecstatic crescendo of:]

"Yes! Rest! Yess! Rest! Yesss! Rest! Rest! Rest!"

CUT TO

SCENE IX

Location: Thomas Edison's bathroom.

[Edison looks at himself in the mirror, heaves a heavy sigh, squats and attempts to sit where there is nothing to sit upon, and tumbles to the floor. Strains of celestial music are heard. For a moment a great light appears above Edison's head. He looks up, becomes inspired with the universal concept of rest, then realizes the immediate need for a device to sit upon. He shouts:]

EDISON:

Clifford! Get in here!

RABBI:

The Archangelic intelligence of Briah then communicates broad general concepts of seating devices to the detail-loving Angel-nerds of Yetzirah. . .

CUT TO

SCENE X

Location: Blueprint room.

[Clifford hurriedly distributes memos to excited nerd angels. Much juvenile squealing and wildly irritating laughter is heard.]

CUT TO

SCENE XI

Location: Furniture warehouse showroom.

[Rabbi is back seated comfortably in the easy chair.]

. . . who finally manage to inspire someone down here in Assiah to quit daydreaming about things and get off their rear ends and actually construct the chair of his or her dreams.

[From his easy chair, Rabbi uses a pointer to indicate the Hebrew letters יהוה *on a nearby blackboard.]*

Yod—Heh—Vau—Heh is the fourfold creative process. It is the formula by which the pure consciousness of the Deity (Yod) descends into matter (Heh Final). From our point of view down here in Assiah, it appears like the wonder of creation.

You might think that, from the Deity's point of view, this creative process appears to be a depressing degeneration of energy and power. But I don't think that is the case.

Remember the Third Command-Rant—There really isn't a creation, time or space, Heaven or Earth—because the ultimate reality resides not in Assiah...

[Pointing to the letter Heh Final יהו ֻה *]*

...or Yetzirah...

[Pointing to the letter Vau יה ֻו ה *]*

...or Briah...

[Pointing to the letter Heh יֻ הוה *]*

...But right here in Yodland...

[Pointing to the letter Yod יְהוִה *]*

    …Atziluth, the environment of pure and infinite conscious-ness—infinite bliss. The other worlds are as unreal as your shadow.

[Rabbi pulls three pair of sunglasses out of his pocket and puts them on, one over the other.]

    Assiah is like looking at the Sun with three pairs of sunglasses. The Material World is just the heaviest, slowest, and grossest aspects of the Divine light.

[Takes off one pair of sunglasses.]

    We see more in Yetzirah…

[Takes off another pair of sunglasses.]

    …and Briah is much brighter but…

[Takes off last pair of sunglasses.]

    But those three worlds are just the distorted image of the real thing.

[Rabbi rests back in the easy chair and closes his eyes. Camera slowly zooms in on his peaceful face as he falls asleep in the easy chair.]

[At extreme close-up, image blurs completely, then refocuses on Rabbi's face, then pulls back to reveal Rabbi's dead body lying on its back on a dissection table in a morgue. Segue to Qabalistic Autopsy Sketch.]

•   •   •

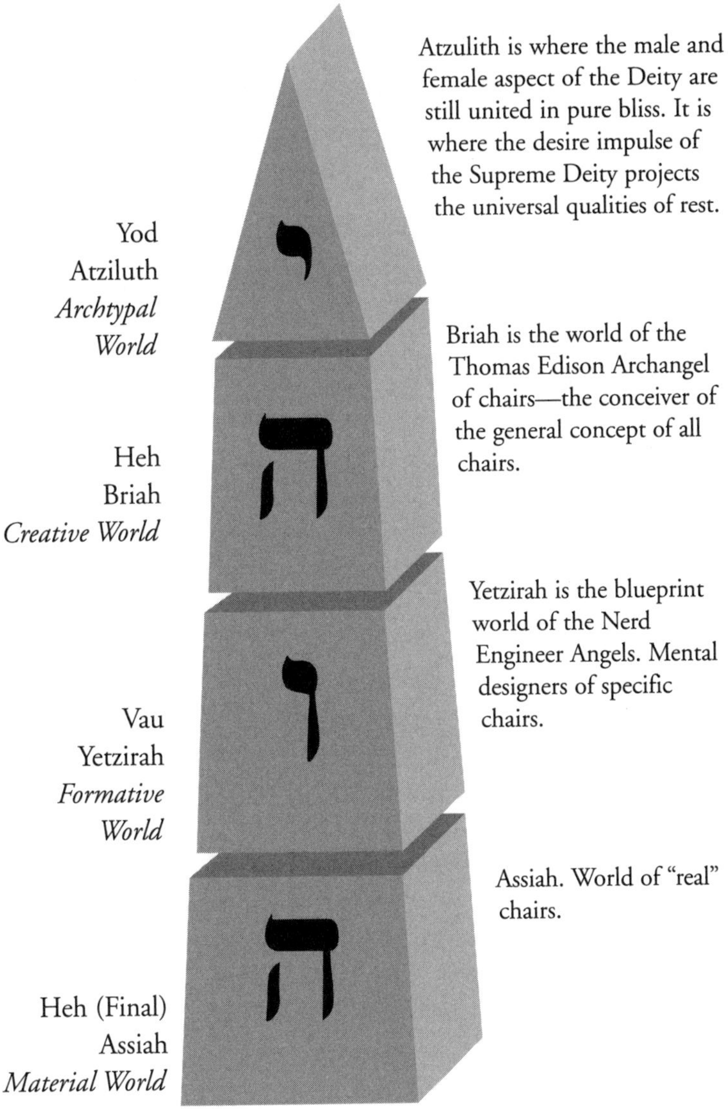

Atzulith is where the male and female aspect of the Deity are still united in pure bliss. It is where the desire impulse of the Supreme Deity projects the universal qualities of rest.

Yod
Atziluth
Archtypal
World

Briah is the world of the Thomas Edison Archangel of chairs—the conceiver of the general concept of all chairs.

Heh
Briah
Creative World

Yetzirah is the blueprint world of the Nerd Engineer Angels. Mental designers of specific chairs.

Vau
Yetzirah
Formative
World

Assiah. World of "real" chairs.

Heh (Final)
Assiah
Material World

Figure 9. Four Qabalistic Worlds.

PART II

The Four Parts of the Soul
Sketch: The Qabalistic Autopsy

SCENE I

Location: Operating room of morgue; Rabbi's body on table.
[Music: Organ, Hymn, "Abide with Me."]

RABBI *[voice over]*:

Then shall the dust return to Earth as it was, and the spirit return unto God who gave it.

[Music stops. As Rabbi narrates, camera slowly pans his body from toe to head (for modesty's sake his genital area and the genital areas of his tattoos are marked off with black tape).]

I really look natural, don't I? This is a dissection room of the Qabalistic morgue, and I have volunteered my body for a little demonstration of the four parts of the soul.

Because humans are "made in the image" of the Deity, we reflect the same dynamics as our huge and eternal counterpart. Each of us is a four story Yod, Heh, Vau, Heh, with our own little Atziluth, Briah, Yetzirah and Assiah right here inside us—four parts of our soul which Qabalists refer to as (starting at the top) Chiah, Neshamah, Ruach, and Nephesh. Like the Qabalistic worlds, the three lower parts of the soul are just the distorted image of our real identity, Chiah, the life-force itself.

RABBI:

The lowest part of the soul, which corresponds to Assiah, the

Material World, is called the Nephesh—animal vitality or the animal soul.

The physical body is not really the Nephesh, but the veil of the Nephesh. I call it Nephesh crust. As science advances and we learn more and more about the neural-electrical-magnetic nature of the body, it gets harder to determine where the crust leaves off and the Nephesh begins. Let's just say for starters that the Nephesh is that primitive level of consciousness that we share with the animal kingdom—our instincts, our primitive appetites, emotions and sex drive, our survival mechanisms. We can observe the Nephesh manifest most clearly in individuals who, because of unfortunate circumstances, are deprived of the proper function of the rational mind. We can also spot it in ourselves in moments of blind rage, or when we are so frightened of a fire we jump out the window of a 16-story building, or when we get so horny we forget this fling will ruin our lives.

Wild and dangerous as the Nephesh can be, it makes each of us complete—an accurate reflection of the greater spiritual reality—it is where we live—it is our personal Assiah and every angel in the celestial realms would give its right wing to own one.

[Morgue Doctor in surgical clothes moves into the picture. She takes a scalpel from the instrument tray and moves toward the Rabbi's head. Camera zooms in on the neck area, as the scalpel blade nears the throat. Camera moves away before any incision is made.]

The part of the soul that corresponds to Yetzirah, the Formative World, is called the Ruach—the intellect. Just as the physical body is the crust of the Nephesh, the Nephesh forms the crust of the Ruach.

•   •   •

SCENE II

Location: Medical Laboratory, complete with Bunsen burners, glass tubing, and electronic instruments.

[Special effects: Rabbi's severed head is sitting up on its neck facing the camera. It is resting in a shallow laboratory pan half-filled with liquid. Several tubes lead from the liquid to bubbling beakers. Rabbi's head opens its eyes and now becomes the narrator.]

RABBI'S HEAD:

Don't try this at home. This is just a cheap trick to introduce us to the next part of our soul, the Ruach.

Above the Nephesh, corresponding to the world of Yetzirah and the Vau of the Tetragrammaton, is the Ruach—the Intellect and the vehicle of Self-awareness. Now, obviously my physical head and brain are not the real Ruach, because all organic things are too gross to qualify for Ruach-hood. But as you look at my head here in this laboratory pan, I want you to think.

If your feet and your legs were amputated, you would still be you, right? And if your arms were amputated, wouldn't you still consider yourself you? Provided science could keep you alive, how much of your body could be amputated or removed before you would lose your you-ness?

You might answer you would still be you as long as you can think and maintain consciousness of yourself.

But that's the big Ruach lie! Thinking and consciousness are not the same thing—not the same thing at all.

The Ruach part of your soul monopolizes your attention to such a degree that you identify yourself completely with the thinking process. Descartes fell for this hook, line, and sinker when he said "Cogito ergo sum—I think, therefore I am." Ultimately, the real you doesn't need the "think" part of the equation to "maintain consciousness." Even if you could no longer "think" there would still be "you" and there would still be "consciousness." The Ruach part of your soul, however, is incapable of grasping that subtle fact. It is unable to transcend itself to imagine a self without thinking.

Like a narcissistic and domineering mother, Ruach consumes your full attention—causing you to *think* about life rather than live it—seek *understanding* rather than enlightenment—*comprehension* rather than bliss.

[Morgue Doctor again moves into the picture. She picks up a power drill. Camera zooms in on the Rabbi's head as the Doctor places the drill-tip directly to his forehead at the area of the third eye. Camera moves away before the drilling begins. The Rabbi's head continues his narration over the sound of the drilling.]

The part of the soul that corresponds to Briah, the Creative World and the Heh of the Tetragrammaton, is called the Neshamah—the seat of our Transcendent Awareness. Just as the physical body is the crust of the Nephesh, and the Nephesh forms the crust of the Ruach, the Ruach forms the crust of the Neshamah.

[Special effects: The camera enters the darkness of the neatly drilled hole in the Rabbi's forehead.]

RABBI:

Practitioners of ceremonial magick often argue with each other over the question, "Are angels, demons, spirits, and other magical phenomena objective or subjective realities? Do they exist outside of us or are they just in our heads?"

The answer is simple. The spirits and every other denizen of objective reality are all in your head—only—you have no idea how infinitely huge your head is!

• • •

SCENE III

Location: Interior Rabbi's head—a cozy den with a modest fireplace before which we find a golden retriever asleep on a braided rug, and the Rabbi reclined in an easy chair. He is calmly smoking a pipe. His eyes are closed, but the brow of his forehead is furrowed as if he is in profound thought or mystical reverie. He never opens his eyes but continues his narration in voice-over.

RABBI:

> The Neshamah, the Thomas Edison Archangel part of your soul, is the Soul Intuition. It is our Transcendent Awareness, that part of us that rises above the thinking process and vibrates in greater harmony with the ultimate reality. We can't really understand the Neshamah because the machinery of our thoughts is based in Ruach, and can only take in so much information before going into overload and breaking down.
>
> For our illustration here, we view my Neshamah as being centered inside my physical skull. It may or may not be centered there, but there is one thing for certain—the Neshamah part of our soul reaches infinitely farther than the confines of our physical body. As a matter of fact, for all intents and purposes, the scope of the Neshamah is infinite. It is in touch with energies and levels of consciousness our Ruach would not understand even if it could conceive of them.
>
> We have all heard stories of mothers, separated from their children by hundreds or thousands of miles, knowing instinctively when their young one's are in danger. Is this because at the traumatic moment the child emits some kind of signal is that telegraphed across the ocean to the mother? No! It is because the mother's Neshamah is so huge the child can never escape it, no matter how many miles separate their physical bodies.

A mother's intuition is only a very primitive example of this Transcendent Awareness. It is clear to me that if it were possible to understand the scope and potential of the human Neshamah we could solve many of the mysteries surrounding the so-called "supernatural" events of religious traditions and the unanswered questions of modern psychic research.

The highest part of the soul that corresponds to Atziluth, the Archetypal World, and the Yod of the Tetragrammaton, is called the Chiah. It is the undiluted Life-Force itself, and it is our true identity. All the other parts of the soul are veils of the Chiah. Just as the physical body is the crust of the Nephesh, and the Nephesh forms the crust of the Ruach, and the Ruach forms the crust of the Neshamah—the Neshamah forms the crust of the Chiah. If we found the Neshamah hard to talk about, our Chiah is even more challenging.

[Special effects: The camera backs up to reveal that the entire scene of the interior of the Rabbi's head is only an image on a television screen. A hand, holding a remote clicker comes into view. The hand aims the clicker at the television and pushes a button. The television screen changes to the blank and snowy image found in between channels.]

[Over the white noise of the blank screen the Rabbi continues his voice-over narration.]

RABBI:

We've all seen this snowy image and heard this irritating hiss whenever we tune in a television channel that isn't carrying a broadcast signal. Astronomers now tell us that what we are seeing and hearing is nothing more or less than the radiation echo of the Big Bang itself, which emanates hauntingly from the empty space between the stars. If we personified this unimaginable energy as a God, it would dwarf to insignificance all the lesser forces and beings in the celestial family. Such is the nature of the Chiah when compared to the other parts of the soul.

Yod—Heh—Vau—Heh
Atziluth—Briah—Yetzirah—Assiah
Chiah—Neshamah—Ruach—Nephesh

The Nephesh lives but is not self-aware. The Ruach is self-aware and aware the self is living. The Neshamah is the essence of life's awareness, but the Chiah is Life itself, the soul's true identity.

If there is any purpose for our incarnations, it is to perfectly integrate the four parts of our soul so that we can function as perfect units of the supreme consciousness and uninhibitedly manifest that consciousness on all planes of existence.

[Special effects: The hand, holding a remote clicker, comes again into view. The hand aims the clicker at the television and pushes a button. The television goes dark except for the tiny white dot in the center of the screen. White dot slowly fades to black.]

The End

Yod
Chiah
Life-Force

Heh
Neshamah
Soul Intuition

Vau
Ruach
Intellect

Heh (Final)
Nepesh
Animal Soul

The Chiah is Life-Force itself. It is our true identity, which for all intents and purposes, is identical with the consciousness of pure Deity.

The Neshamah is the part of our soul that transcends the thinking process and vibrates in greater harmony with the ultimate reality.

The Ruach is our intellect. It is the part of our soul that monopolizes our attention to such a degree that we identify ourselves completely with the thinking process.

The Nephesh is the primitive level of consciousness we share with the animal kingdom—instincts, primitive appetites, emotions, and sex drive—survival mechanisms.

Figure 10. Four Parts of the Soul.

7

THE TREE OF LIFE

Introduced by Lon Milo DuQuette

The light of Kether is One. It is pure consciousness. Its radiance never diminishes. The nine Sephiroth beneath it simply separate and filter the light. This trickle-down consciousness, not some mythological fruit-eating incident, is the real "Fall of Man."
—RABBI LAMED BEN CLIFFORD

To Chicken Qabalists (and other modern students who presume a more exalted opinion of themselves), the schematic image known as the Tree of Life is the most recognizable symbol of Qabalah. Esteemed as it is, this diagram of the anatomy of God is by no means the most ancient[1] Qabalistic device, but its components (the 10 primal emanations of creation, or Sephiroth,[2] and the 22 paths that connect them) display with remarkable simplicity the most important and venerable principles of Qabalistic doctrine.

Although the Tree of Life, as such, is not mentioned in the Sepher Yetzirah,[3] it is the visual elaboration of the fundamental statement of that great text that informs us that "Deity created the universe in 32 mysterious paths of wisdom—10 Sephiroth out of nothing and 22 letters."

How did the author(s) of the Sepher Yetzirah reach the conclusion that 10 Sephiroth out of nothing and 22 letters were the vehicles of divine creation? Most certainly it was an oral tradition predating the Sepher Yetzirah, but it had to have originated somewhere. Predictably Rabbi Ben Clifford had the answer, and this chapter is dedicated to his thoughts on the matter.

What follows are transcriptions and notes from two long-suppressed tape recordings made by Ben Clifford in 1978 and 1979. During the period of his public ministry, these early tapes, and the so-called documents that accompanied them, posed somewhat of an embarrassment to his students who believed, with good reason, that if they were made public Ben Clifford's reputation would be irreparably damaged. The source of this concern stemmed not from the content of the material (which, as we shall soon see, is rich in Qabalistic wisdom), but from the incredulous format of the presentation.

It appears the Rabbi would actually have us believe that he possessed original "essays" written over twenty-five hundred years ago by students of the Zerubbabel Institute of Philosophical Youth. I am sure I do not have to tell the reader that Ben Clifford is again having us on in this matter. But please don't let this literary device tempt you to dismiss the value of these little compositions. They are some of the most ingenious examples of Qabalistic logic I have ever seen displayed. I find it quite easy to believe that, sometime in the distant past, the fundamental elements of the Qabalah were developed in a manner not too dissimilar to that outlined by these imaginary students.

Sacred Numbers and the Creation of the Tree of Life

EDITED FROM THE TRANSCRIPTIONS AND NOTES OF
THE TAPE-RECORDED PRESENTATIONS OF
RABBI LAMED BEN CLIFFORD

GOOD MORNING MY FRIENDS. Please help yourselves to coffee and doughnuts. Today's presentation is a very special one (I'm even tape recording it), so I want you all to stay awake. I am very excited about today's lecture and I think you should be, too. Not only are we going to learn about sacred numbers and the creation of the Tree of Life, we are first going to discover some astounding things concerning the history of this beloved institution. So, let's take our seats and quiet down. *(Unintelligible question from a student.)* Yes, but please keep your socks on.

I am often asked, "Rabbi Ben Clifford, you speak often of the Zerubbabel Institute of Philosophical Youth, yet we see no buildings, find no trace of such an organization in the directories of schools, or even the telephone directory. Is not Z.I.P.Y. a child of your own imagination?" Well, dear friends, mock and scoff as you will, you need look no further than the sacred scriptures themselves. Behold! It is written in the eleventh chapter of the Book of Ezra.[4] (A facsimile of this page is reproduced for interested readers on page 108.)

CHAPTER 11

AND it came to pass in the second year following the completion of the Second Temple, that Ezra, priest of Israel, decreed that a school should be builded for the purpose of discovering all there was to know about God, human beings, the universe, and life in general.

2. This proclamation caused great consternation among the children of Israel and government leaders.

3. "What will it profit us to gain this knowledge? How shall we pay for such an undertaking? Does Ezra think we are rich like Hittites?"

4. Indeed, the enterprise seemed doomed for, although the citizens were sincere and pious and revered the wisdom of Ezra, none among them could justify in their hearts the expenditure of precious resources for such an obscure and intangible endeavor.

5. But Ezra was wise as a serpent. He realized that the essence of God (if God be truly God), must be reflected in every unit of creation.

6. It followed that if one meditated long enough and hard enough about anything, sooner or later the Deity would reveal Itself therein!

7. He took counsel with his publisher, Nut & Geb of West Jericho (who during the dark years of the Babylonian captivity published his controversial *"Pentateuch: The Five Books of Moses"*), and he also supped with the Chief Financial Officer of the Memphis Papyrus Company.

8. He vowed to these great men of commerce that if they subsidized this holy institution, he would guarantee that their edition of the *Pentateuch* would forever be used as the primary text at the school.

9. Furthermore, he took the shoe from off his foot and rent his sock and spat upon the palms of his hands and swore a solemn oath that he would enter into an exclusive covenant with Nut & Geb to supply *Pentateuchs* in deluxe editions to the school in perpetuity.

Marginal references:

CHAP. 11
Ezra 7:6

Or *Zen*

Deu 34:3

2 Ki 24:12

Hsa 9:6
1 Ki 15:5

Or *Meteorites*

Or *Bribeth be them*

Or *Cheapeth*
Rth 7:4
Gen 13:15

Or *Sweetheart deal*

Isa 30:6
Gen 1:27

Figure 11. From the Book of Ezra.

Thus, more than 2,500 years ago, was born the Zerubbabel Institute of Philosophical Youth, or Z.I.P.Y., and you, my dear students, are the inheritors of that proud tradition.

Let's imagine that we are the first students of that great Qabalistic school. We are not sure how we got here. Perhaps we earned a scholarship. Perhaps our fathers are wealthy, or members of the Jerusalem Chamber of Commerce, or they are government or temple officials. Regardless of how we came to be here, our assignment is simple. We are to *think* about things—all day—all night.

To focus our considerations, and to give us scaffolding upon which to perform our mental gymnastics, our teachers have provided us with a single text, *The Pentateuch: The Five Books of Moses.*[5] We are told that these writings are holy, and if we apply ourselves diligently, every mystery of Heaven and Earth will reveal itself to us in these pages.

"But sir?" a learned student might have injected, "I've read the Pentateuch scores of times, and the mysteries of Heaven and Earth have not revealed themselves to me."

"Then, my son," our teacher might have answered, "You must seek them—one sentence, one word, one letter at a time. If that doesn't work, you are to read the texts backward, count the words, count the characters, transpose, transfer, translate, transliterate, shuffle and braid the letters—skin, dissect, magnify, synonymize, antonymize, homonymize them until your brain explodes. Only then can your mind purge itself of the false reality of contradiction. Then and only then will the pure wisdom of God flood into your vacuous skull to fill the void."

"But sir? If God made everything and His essence pervades everything then would not examination and meditation upon any text, indeed any *thing* whatsoever reward us with the same spiritual enlightenment?

"Yes, my son, you are absolutely correct. But the fact remains we have entered into an exclusive covenant with the publishing house of Nut & Geb to supply *Pentateuchs in deluxe editions to the school in perpetuity.*"

Of course there is no way of telling whether or not such a conversation ever took place between student and teacher. However, there is no ambiguity about the documents I hold in my hand.[6] They are over twenty-five hundred years old and were obtained at great expense from a reputable antiquities dealer in New Orleans. They are nothing less than authentic remnants of actual classroom material from the Zerubbabel Institute of Philosophical Youth.

As luck would have it, these papers all deal with the evolution of the concept of the Tree of Life. I can think of no better way of showing the art of Qablistic thinking in action than to reproduce this rare and historic material in its entirety.

Rare Official Classroom Papers
Zerubbabel Institute
of Philosophical Youth

CLASS: QABALISTIC THINKING 101
CLASSMASTER: RABBI MILTON ROE
CLASS No. 1   DATE: ADAR, 23RD, 520 B.C.[7]

TEXT FOR MEDITATION:
> *"And created the Elohim Adam in the image of Elohim created they them, male and female created they them."*
> —Genesis, I:27

POSTULATE: Each one of us is made in the image of the Deity.

ASSIGNMENT No 1: Think about yourself—then write a 300-word essay on the creative nature of God.

Winning Essay No. 1
Submitted by Shechaniah, the son of Jehiel

When Rabbi Roe gave us the assignment to think about ourselves and then write an essay on the creative nature of God, I was sure I would not be able to do it, but then I started to think—the text says the Elohim created Adam (or the human race) in the image of the Elohim. We are not told that snakes, or aardvarks, or fish, or worms, or any other animals or plants were created in the image of the Elohim.

It seems to me that the question that begs asking is: "What separates human beings from other animals?" I think I have the answer, at least I have *an* answer.

Thumbs! We have thumbs!

Sure, apes and monkeys and a few lemurs have thumbs, but none of them use them to create things. The fact that our thumb opposes the other four fingers is one very important thing that separates us from the rest of our animal neighbors. With the opposable thumb our ancestors made weapons, harnessed fire, fashioned tools and implements, created works of art, and hitch-hiked. Our hands make us creative beings (just like the Deity), and the thumb is the key to our hand's success. Therefore I have made the following conclusions:

♦ The "hand" of the Creator (or the creative mechanics of the universe) must be an absolute *unity* (represented by the thumb), and that It executes Its creative power through a *fourfold* process (represented by the four fingers). This, I believe, is the primary reason our venerable ancestors worshiped *one* God whose great Name is composed of *four* letters,[8] י ה ו ה.

♦ The Hebrew word for "hand" is י ו ד YOD. Yod is the 10th letter of the Hebrew alphabet and the fundamental letter of the alphabet. As my father taught me, *"Yod is a flame. Blow upon it and you form all the other letters of the alphabet."* Yod represents the number 10 in our system of counting. Furthermore, we can see that the holy number 4 itself conceals the number 10 (1 + 2 + 3 + 4 = 10).

Conclusion:

After meditating upon myself and my hand I conclude that there is *one* God who creates through a *four*fold process and ultimately manifests through *ten* levels of expression. For this reason, I contend that the numbers ONE, FOUR, and TEN be considered holy and of primary importance in our study.

Final Note:
Dear Dr. Roe,
This essay is 398 words in length. Do I get extra credit?
                                    —Shechaniah, the son of Jehiel

---

Winning Essay No. 2
Submitted by Ramiah, the son of Jeziah

I am sure I speak for the entire class when I say that I am filled with great admiration for my classmate, Shechaniah the son of Jehiel, whose dissertation yesterday on the creative nature of God was a thrilling display of logic and insight. I agree wholeheartedly with all his conclusions and wish to use them as the foundation of further discussion.

I think we can all agree that the creative power of the human hand, with its opposable thumb, is a key characteristic that separates humans from other forms of terrestrial life. It is also very logical that we, being created in the image of God, should conclude that God is an absolute monad who executes Its creative power through a fourfold process. This supports our tradition of the Four Qabalistic Worlds[9] which are mirrored in humans by the Four Parts of the Soul,[10] and should earn our veneration for the numbers ONE and FOUR. Brother Shechaniah also pointed out that, because the word Yod (hand) is the tenth letter of the sacred Hebrew Alphabet, and that Yod represents the number 10, we should hold the number TEN in high regard as well. Also, we must remember that we have two hands, with a total of ten fingers, and this fact further underscores the importance of the number TEN.

I now wish to point out that the word Yod (YVD ד ו י) spelled in full (Y י = 10, V ו = 6, D ד = 4) adds to the number TWENTY, which reminds us that we (and therefore God) have twenty digits, for, as the wise cobbler said, we mustn't forget our toes.

Now you may ask, "Is TWENTY as significant and as holy a number as ONE or FOUR or TEN?" I say no, because our ten toes, while providing certain symmetry to our bodies, do not exactly set us apart from other less spiritually endowed creatures. But in between our two sets of fingers there is one thing that does.

Our tongue! We have a tongue—the power of speech! Through speech we communicate and inform—just as the Deity does! Through speech we create images in our minds and in the minds of others—just as the Deity does! Through speech we give names to all things in our environment and organize our thoughts—just as the Deity does! Through speech we bless and curse our friends and enemies—just as the Deity does! Through speech we command, subjugate, and exploit anyone whose will is weaker than our own—just as Deity does!

Finally, between our two sets of toes is another member that actually gives us the power to create other human beings in our own image. True, humans are not the only creatures who reproduce. But our father Abraham entered into a covenant with the Deity, a covenant sealed by a curious gesture of mutilation. The rite of circumcision not only symbolizes our obedience to our God, but also our acknowledgment to ourselves that we can master and control our sexual drives for the greater good of family, our race, and humanity in general.

Conclusion:

I think we all can agree that our unique powers of speech, and the godlike power of creation (that both men and women carry in their loins), certainly qualify as divine characteristics, and elevate the marvelous number TWENTY-TWO to equal status with ONE, FOUR, and TEN. As our holy Hebrew alphabet is composed of 22 letters, I think there can be no debate on this matter.

—Ramiah, the son of Jeziah

ASSIGNMENT NO. 2: Role-Playing Exercise.

You are the Deity. You have not yet created anything.
How would you go about making everything in the
universe out of your Oneness?

EXTRA CREDIT: Discover other Holy Numbers.

Winning Essay No. 1
Submitted by Zabad, the son of Aziza

After studying the last few winning essays, I have to confess that I'm
a little embarrassed to share the fruits of my meditations. I don't
come from the big city like most of my fellow students, and so I guess
the wheels of my mind naturally seek out the ruts of homier byways
of deliberation.

All I know is that if I were the Deity before creation, I must have
been very lonely. Being the only and absolute Being, I might not even
realize the nature of my own self. I symbolize this pre-creational state
as a simple circle (I have chosen this figure because a circle has no
beginning or end) and designate it by the holy number ONE.

Figure 12. The Holy Number 1.

Now, since I am ONE and absolute, it follows that ONE is the only
real number—the only legitimate reality. As the Deity, I think I
would be quite happy in my condition of oneness, and leave it at
that, but something clearly happened to induce me to create. In order

for me to create the many things in the universe, I would need to create more numbers. I think it happened like this:

I was alone and bored, and began to ponder the nature of myself. "What am I?" This was difficult because I was the only ONE. I had nothing else with which to compare myself. I wasn't a "this" or a "that" because I had not yet created "thises" or "thats." I was the absolute, there was no "outside" of me. I could not hold up a mirror and look at my image and say, "Oh look! I'm one of those!" I could, however, with great stillness and concentration, turn the focus of my attention inward and, like the holy men of India, observe my perfect reflection at the very center of my being. I would then for the first time be conscious of myself. "I am *this*!" I would shout.

Even instantly, as these words echoed in my absoluteness, I would fall from my pristine state of singularity, for I would now have to admit the concept of TWO:

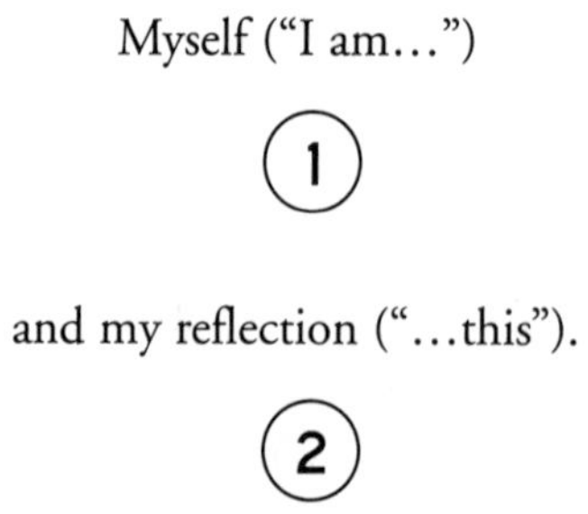

Myself ("I am...")

①

and my reflection ("...this").

②

Figure 13. The concept of two.

Oh! Curse the moment I ever brought TWO into existence, because the moment my Self became conscious of my reflection (my Not-Self), a third concept was created, that is . . . the *knowledge* of the *difference* between Self and Not-Self. "I am 'this' but 'that' is not I."

Figure 14. The concept of three.

Conclusion:

I assert that creation commenced when the Deity stirred from undistracted ecstasy and became self-conscious, an act which transformed Its self-*existence* (as the inscrutable Divine Unity) into Its self-*image* (as the Deity of creation). Therefore, I suggest that we also consider the number THREE one of our primary holy numbers.

—Zabad, the son of Aziza

Winning Essay No. 2
Submitted by Jozabad, the son of Shimei
Adar, 28th, 520 B.C.

My compliments to Zabad, the son of Aziza, for his wonderful essay on the Holy number THREE. I'm sure he would have gone on to enlighten us further had he not been in such a hurry last night to slink off to West Bethany, so he could "accidentally" bump into someone else's girlfriend at a "certain" off-limits inn and ply her with pomegranate fizzes, while his classmates stayed up late working on this assignment.

Be that as it may, my self-control and dedication to study has rewarded me with the following:

Since TWO and THREE are merely attributes of ONE, they should be considered along with the number ONE as a *Trinity Unit*.

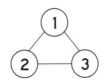

Figure 15. The trinity.

The Trinity Unit then behaves in precisely the same manner as the original ONE did when it reflected itself to become TWO. It reflects itself to create a second Trinity Unit:

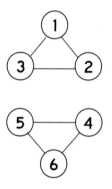

Figure 16. The second trinity.

A third Trinity Unit is instantly created in the same way that the original THREE was instantly created upon the birth of TWO:

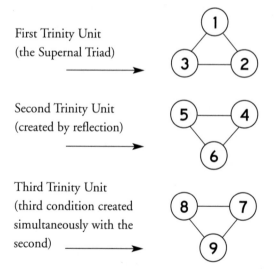

First Trinity Unit
(the Supernal Triad)

Second Trinity Unit
(created by reflection)

Third Trinity Unit
(third condition created
simultaneously with the
second)

Figure 17. The third trinity.

Conclusion:

As Zabad concluded, creation commences when the Deity defines itself and becomes self-conscious—a three-part act which defines ONE as an abstract and unmanifested Trinity (the Supernal Triad). But what Zabad was apparently too distracted to realize was that the Deity cannot stop at self-knowledge. Momentum has been established which will result in a further series of six phenomenal emanations by which the universe will categorize itself and organize its infinite potentialities. The following diagram will illustrate this idea.

The Divine Light first *projects* from the Supernal Triad,

then *shatters* like sunlight through a prism and filters through the next six descending emanations,

until it finally *manifests* (from our point of view) on the material plane—Earth—number TEN.

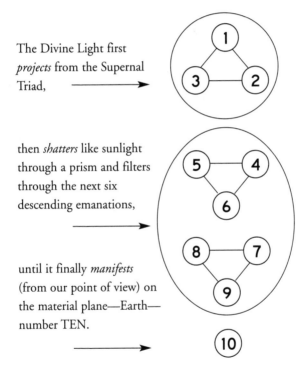

Figure 18. Projection, Shattering, and Manifestation of the Divine Light.

I believe that TEN hangs from the three Triads like a cosmic dingleberry and provides an environment—a *Kingdom*—that traps the diffused and crystallized divine light inside a prison of matter. We live in this Kingdom. It is the lowest of the emanations. It is where the Divine Light vibrates at its lowest frequency. It is where the invisible becomes visible.

—Jozabad, the son of Shimei

Winning Essay No. 3
Submitted by Zabad, the son of Aziza

I abase myself before my esteemed colleague Jozabad, the son of Shimei, for his stunning demonstration of spiritual insight. I hereby propose that his diagram arrangement of the 10 emanations or Sephiroth be known from this day forward as "THE TEN NUMBERED BUBBLES OF JOZABAD."

With all due respect to my friend's genius, however, I would like to point out a few important aspects of his ten bubbles that, in his flurry to ennoble himself in the eyes of the faculty, have escaped his attention.

When we look at all ten steps of creation, we see that the TENTH emanation is the reflection of the NINTH, which is the reflection of the SIXTH, which is the reflection of the ONE.

It is as if the divine light of God

is reflected and made manifest upon the Sun

which is reflected upon the Moon

which is reflected upon Earth.

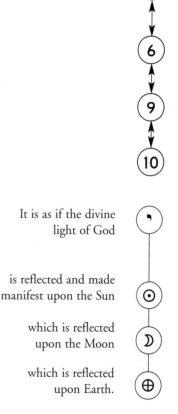

Figure 19. The steps of creation.

To form the backbone of the Ten Numbered Bubbles of Jozabad, the numbers ①, ⑥, ⑨, and ⑩ are as critical to the structure of the universe as the spine is to the human body. They are also indicative of the four letters of the name of Diety ה ו ה י (Yod-Heh-Vau-Heh) and all that It represents in the universe and the human soul.[11] If the class has any doubt about this, let me point out that the sum of ①, ⑥, ⑨, and ⑩ equals 26, the same as the supreme name of God ה ו ה י.

Furthermore (and most importantly I believe), when we insert the three paths that join ①, ⑥, ⑨, and ⑩, we create a total of 12 paths. (I call them Zabad's Twelve Paths of Glory.) These 12 paths link the 10 emanations and bring the total steps of creation to the sacred number TWENTY-TWO!

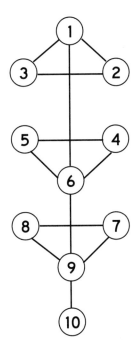

Figure 20. The 12 Paths.

Conclusion:

I believe that I have succeeded in demonstrating how the Deity (1) through the medium of 4, 10, and 22, created the universe and the nature of reality as we perceive it. I think it should be obvious to Rabbi Roe and the entire class that I have mastered the assignment and have wrenched all the wisdom that can be extracted from this line of thinking. I suggest we now move on to another subject, like when do we go co-ed?

—Zabad, the son of Aziza

Grand Prize Winning Essay
Submitted by Ramiah, the son of Jeziah

Once again I am stunned at the intelligence and wisdom exhibited by my classmates, especially the fruits of the recent exchanges between Zabad, the son of Aziza, and Jozabad, the son of Shimei. I most humbly confess that my feeble mind could never have developed the Ten Numbered Bubbles of Jozabad, or Zabad's Twelve Paths of Glory. Please know that anything I might add at this point must only be viewed as my dwarfish mental stature standing upon the shoulders of these two giants.

Still, I must strenuously disagree with Zabad's assertion that we have concluded our meditation on the diagram that he and Jozabad have labored so diligently to erect. As I was the first in the class to draw our attention to the holiness of the number 22, I must respectfully point out certain flaws in Zabad's thinking concerning his "Twelve Paths of Glory." I will begin by pointing out that I believe there are two additional pillars that flank the middle pillar (figure 21).

As it is postulated, each one of us is made in the image of the Deity. These two pillars correspond to the right and left side of the human body (the middle pillar being the spine). They also accommodate the entire spectrum of universal opposites that so profoundly

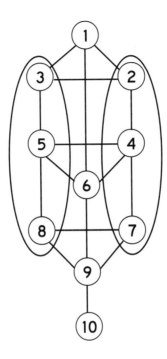

Figure 21. Note the two additional "pillars."

divide our perception of reality; light-darkness, male-female, strength-weakness, the middle pillar serving to balance and harmonize these extremes.

Furthermore, I believe that the paths which join the 10 Sephiroth are not merely nails that attach the emanations, but are actually conduits of divine intelligence, which transmit the influence of each Sephirah back and forth between its neighbor. Consequently, all the Sephiroth should be joined by paths (shown in figure 22 on page 124).

You will notice in my diagram that I have drawn broken paths leading from 3 to 4 and from 2 to 5. *This is because I believe that these paths* do not *exist*. To explain this, we must return for a moment to Zabad's earlier essay, which explained how ONE became THREE. If

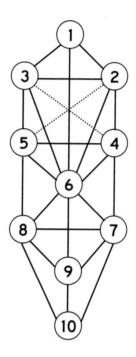

Figure 22. All Sephiroth are joined.

you recall, he wrote that ONE is the only real number. TWO is just a projected reflection of ONE, and THREE merely a condition of recognition that TWO is not ONE.

So, too, ① ② ③ is the only real Triad; the Triad of ④ ⑤ ⑥ is only its reflection, and the third Triad is merely the replication of the second. The area between the first Triad and the second Triad is like the impenetrable surface of a mirror. It is an inscrutable *Abyss*.

As I gaze into the mirror hanging on the wall in my dormitory room, I see my reflection, an unreal image of the real me in my real room. So it is with the Deity. The Supernal Triad (① ② ③) is the *real* thing existing on the *real* side of the mirror/Abyss. On the *unreal* side of the Abyss are all the unreal things (including you and me and everything we perceive in the universe). They assume a semblance of reality because they, like my reflection in the mirror, are bound by the *image* of the real supernal patterns and forms.

Just as I give a kind of life to my reflection in the mirror, so all the manifold units of creation are vivified by the Living Light of the Supernal Triad. Indeed, that Light is our true identity. What we think is our body, our world, our self, is only the shadowy reflection of the Divine Being whose radiance shattered at the Abyss. We aren't even truly alive, we are just the reflection of real life. "And created the Elohim Adam in the *image* of Elohim created they them, male and female created they them."

Just as we cannot walk into a room reflected in a mirror, a path cannot exist between ③ of the Supernal Triad and ④ of the second Triad. Other paths appear to cross the Abyss, but they aren't really Paths, but either *reflected* paths or avenues of *reflection*:

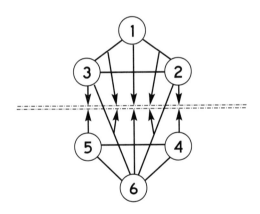

Figure 23. Reflecting paths.

♦ The path joining ① and ⑥ is the avenue of reflection between ① and ⑥.

♦ The path joining ② and ④ is the avenue of reflection between ② and ④.

- ◆ The path joining ③ and ⑤ is the avenue of reflection between ③ and ⑤.

- ◆ The path joining ① and ② is reflected as the path joining ② and ⑥.

- ◆ The path joining ① and ③ is reflected as the path joining ③ and ⑥.

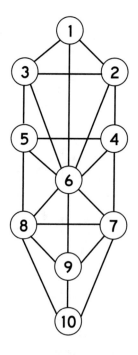

Figure 24. Completed Tree of Life.

Conclusion:
This leaves us with 22 paths joining the 10 Sephiroth. I presume to call the entire thing "Ramiah's 32 Mysterious Paths of Wisdom." It is

my firm belief (although I am not prepared to elucidate further at the moment) that these 22 paths have a direct correspondence with the 22 letters of our sacred Hebrew alphabet. I further contend that the mystery of their placement upon this Tree of Life (as I have also presumed to name it) is the key to eventual return to our original divine estate.

—Ramiah, the son of Jeziah

8

QABALISTIC MAGICK AND THE TREE OF LIFE

Introduced by Lon Milo DuQuette

It's all in your head, you just have no idea how big your head is.
—RABBI LAMED BEN CLIFFORD

To the horror of many in the orthodox community, Rabbi Ben Clifford encouraged his students to learn and practice the magical art of spirit evocation. Also, he made no secret of the fact that he himself, on occasion, conjured demons and spirits to help him address specific personal problems. He taught that summoning spirits to do one's bidding was perfectly compatible with his field-theory, which states, "It's all in your head, you just have no idea how big your head is." He insisted that the successful completion of any act of will was a form of spirit evocation.

Unfortunately, he left no record of his personal workings in this area and, as he never made it a regular part of his course of instruction, very little material could be found to give us a glimpse into this colorful aspect of his spiritual career.

The work that follows was originally written as a postscript to the Z.I.P.Y. papers regarding the genesis of the Tree of Life. It was obviously never intended to serve as a comprehensive treatise on spirit evocation. It does, however, contain an extremely useful hierarchical flow-chart of the Archangels, Angels, Intelligences, and Spirits that clearly outlines who is in charge of who in a Tree of Life universe. The accompanying essay also reveals Ben Clifford's basic attitudes regarding the underlying theory of Qabalistic ceremonial magick and, I believe, should be of immeasurable value to anyone who may wish to embark on such practices.

But before we turn to the essay, I would like us to examine the contents of a short but provocative letter Ben Clifford wrote to an Indiana student in 1988. His letter is in response to several questions the student posed concerning the evocation of spirits of the Goetia.[1]

The Rabbi himself confessed that his answers were gross simplifications. Nevertheless, I know of no better definition of the underlying theory of Qabalistic magick and spirit evocation than his last sentence: "Gods, archangels, angels, spirits, intelligences, and demons are personifications of all our abilities and potential abilities—a wondrous hierarchy of consciousness that represents the subdivisions of our own soul."

Are the spirits good or evil?

Yes, they are good. Yes, they are evil!

Are the spirits real or just imaginary?

Yes, they are real. Yes, they are imaginary.

Are the spirits part of me, or do they live an existence independent of me?

Yes, the spirits are part of you. Yes, to all *appearances,* and for all *practical purposes,* they live an existence independent of you.

Are the spirits dangerous?

Yes, most definitely, spirits are very dangerous.

Can the spirits hurt me?

Yes, most definitely, spirits can hurt you. They hurt you all the time.

Can the spirits ruin my life?

Yes, most definitely, spirits can ruin your life.

Can the spirits kill me?

Yes, most definitely, spirits can kill you.

Can the spirits harm my loved ones, my neighbors, my nation, or the Earth's fragile ecosystem?

Yes! Most definitely! As a matter of fact, there is no atrocity you can imagine, no wickedness you can conceive of, no monstrous act you can picture in your mind that the spirits cannot inflict upon you, your loved ones, your neighbors, the Earth, or the human race. Aren't you sorry you asked?

The most important question is the question you did *not* ask—

Why on Earth would anyone want to have anything to do with such awful and terrible entities?

And the answer is probably the answer you do not want to hear—but here goes:

> Because, until you master these spiritual forces and consciously redirect their unimaginable power to more constructive projects, their wild energies will continue to gush like burning *Drano* through your soul—along every avenue of least resistance large or small. When you are weak—when

you are tired—when you are sick—or stressed, or drunk, or drugged, or jealous, or angry, or hurt, or insulted, or resentful, or in pain, or succumbing to greed, or being flattered, or when you are afraid—*especially when you are afraid*—and they can ruin your life, harm or even kill you and your loved ones, and make your life a living hell.

Of course these are worst-case scenarios. Most of us have enough reign on our spirits to keep us out of prison or the booby hatch. But all of us could do much better—and the world most definitely would be a better place if we all did better.

Let's take another look at your questions that I answered so glibly, and give them just a bit more attention.

Are the spirits good or evil?

Yes, the spirits are good or evil, in the same way electricity is both good and evil depending upon how it is directed.

Are the spirits real or just imaginary?

The spirits are both real and imaginary, but most of us do not realize how real our imagination is.

Are the spirits part of me, or do they live an existence independent of me?

The spirits are inside you, but most of us do not realize (1) how big our insides really are, or (2) how much out of control and seemingly independent the things inside us can be.

For a moment, let's pretend that your brain (and remember, scientists tell us we use only a tiny fraction of our brain's potential) is the source of all your power and ability to do anything. (Of course it isn't. Remember the four parts of the soul and the fact your Neshamah, the Soul Intuition, was incredibly huge, and that it was the part of the soul that enables your mother to freak out whenever you're in trouble, even if you were on the Moon?) But, just for simplicity's sake, let's say all your powers and abilities are functions of the brain.

Because the brain (under this pretend scenario) is the all-powerful director of our being, we could call it the *god* of our lives. This god is a good administrator, and knows how to effectively delegate authority to get things done. However, having no resources outside of itself to draw upon, the brain-god must divide itself into several large departments, creating from itself a board of directors.

One board member controls our logical and deductive processes, another our imagination and artistic sensibilities. Another board member dominates our sleep and dreams, and one quietly interfaces with our nervous systems. These large sections of the brain—these members of the board of directors, are *archangels* who execute the will of the brain-god.

If we were to dissect the archangel areas of the brain, we would discover that within each of them are smaller areas that do more specific jobs within the archangel's province. For instance, within the archangel of logic we would find the area that adds and subtracts and observes and registers the process of cause and effect. We might find within the artistic archangel an area that allows us to appreciate a beautiful painting, or a sector that sounds an alarm when we see a man wearing brown shoes and white socks with a tuxedo. These middle-management subdivisions of the archangelic zones of the brain are *angels*.

Further dividing the brain, we discover that within each of these angelic regions are even smaller areas that control even more specific applications of their angelic department. We could keep dividing and dividing, creating ever smaller ever more specific intelligences, spirits, and yes, even demons.

Magical evocation is merely identifying the specific spirit who accomplishes the task we want accomplished, then activating in descending order the areas of the brain that control it.

Gods, archangels, angels, spirits, intelligences, and demons are personifications of all our abilities and potential abilities—a wondrous hierarchy of consciousness that represents the subdivisions of our own soul.

Spirit Evocation

EDITED FROM THE TRANSCRIPTION AND NOTES OF
TAPE-RECORDED PRESENTATIONS OF
RABBI LAMED BEN CLIFFORD

I'M SURE YOU ALL AGREE with me that the essays by your ancient classmates are truly remarkable and provide great insight into the logical progression of concepts that went into the creation of the Tree of Life. I'm confident that you are all saying to yourselves, "Why, I would have thought of that if I had nothing to do all day but to think about stuff!" However, there are many important and practical aspects of the Tree that were not covered in these documents by the first *ZIPYites*, and so it falls to me to fill in some of the gaps.

Before I go on, however, I want you never to lose sight of the fact that when we talk about the Sephiroth we are talking about levels of consciousness. When I use the term "pure light of Kether" I'm not talking about some big flashlight in the cosmos, I'm talking about the pure omnipresent, omnipotent, omniscient, omni-the-whole-damned-ball-of-wax consciousness of Deity.

Keeping that in mind, we must remember that even before we toyed with the idea of the Tree of Life we pondered three kinds of wonderful Nothing (Ain, Ain Soph, and Ain Soph Aur) that, like some huge and tiny cosmic egg, somehow managed to bring ONE

(Kether, the Crown, the Self of Deity) into existence. The rest of the Sephiroth on the Tree of Life are merely aspects of this ONE. They appear to degenerate in purity as they descend the Tree, but in actuality, this is just an illusion.

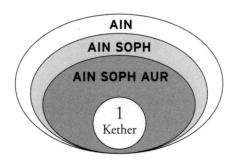

Figure 25. The cosmic egg.

The light of Kether is One. It is pure consciousness. Its radiance never diminishes. The nine Sephiroth beneath it simply separate and filter the light. This trickle-down consciousness, not some mythological fruit-eating incident, is the real "Fall of Man."

In figure 26, we see this process of degeneration projected upon the Tree of Life, and colorfully personified somewhat like a cosmic dysfunctional family.

- ♦ ONE: *Kether* (Crown), the Self of Deity.

- ♦ TWO: *Chokmah* (Wisdom), the Cosmic Father.

- ♦ THREE: *Binah* (Understanding), the Cosmic Mother.

- ♦ FOUR: *Chesed* (Mercy), the expressed Father, paternal, organized, authoritative.

- ♦ FIVE: *Geburah* (Strength), the expressed Mother, active, ferocious, yet nurturing.

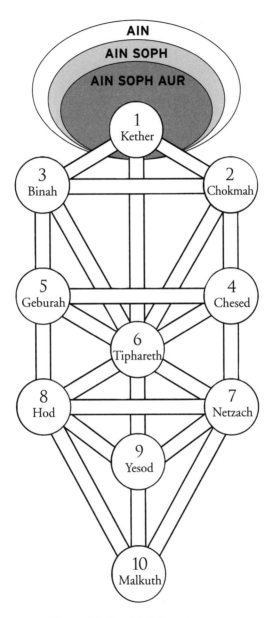

Figure 26. Levels of Consciousness.

- ◆ SIX: *Tiphareth* (Beauty), the Son who is the end result of all these things.

- ◆ SEVEN: *Netzach* (Victory), the degraded Mother, animal emotion.

- ◆ EIGHT: *Hod* (Splendor), the degraded Father, animal reason.

- ◆ NINE: *Yesod* (Foundation), the degraded Son, animal life.

- ◆ TEN: *Malkuth* (Kingdom), the degraded Daughter, the condition of the soul of unenlightened Humanity.

Qabalists further dissect the universe of consciousness by organizing everything into four categories—four Trees of Life. Each Tree corresponds to one of the Four Letters in the Great Divine Name Yod-Heh-Vau-Heh, the four Qabalistic Worlds, and the four parts of the human soul (see figure 27, page 139).

Remember, these are levels of consciousness, and not places or heavens located somewhere out in space. If you are waiting to die so you can go to one of these "higher" planes, you might be very disappointed. Death might not be what you think it is, and there is no reason to believe you will be any smarter than you were when you were alive. Make the effort to attain illumination while you still have a four-part soul.

This Divine pecking order is the corporate flow chart of the universe, and of you and me. The ten segments of Deity in Atziluth rule the ten archangels in Briah, who rule the ten groups of angels in Yetzirah, who rule the various spirits down here in the material plane of Assiah. It's easy to see who rules whom if we imagine the four trees placed one over another, as shown in figure 28 on page 140.

Spirits are the agents who actually do all the heavy lifting on the material plane. You may think you disagree with me on this. You could point out that natural forces, people, and machines seem to be

QABALISTIC WORLD   **PART OF THE SOUL**

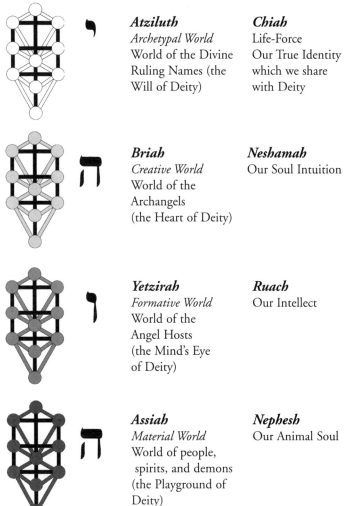

Atziluth
Archetypal World
World of the Divine
Ruling Names (the
Will of Deity)

Chiah
Life-Force
Our True Identity
which we share
with Deity

Briah
Creative World
World of the
Archangels
(the Heart of Deity)

Neshamah
Our Soul Intuition

Yetzirah
Formative World
World of the
Angel Hosts
(the Mind's Eye
of Deity)

Ruach
Our Intellect

Assiah
Material World
World of people,
 spirits, and demons
(the Playground of
Deity)

Nephesh
Our Animal Soul

Figure 27. The Qabalistic Worlds and the human soul.

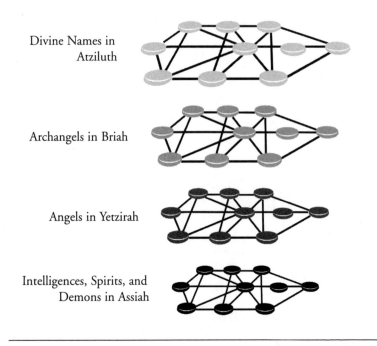

Divine Names in
Atziluth

Archangels in Briah

Angels in Yetzirah

Intelligences, Spirits, and
Demons in Assiah

Figure 28. The Divine Pecking Order.

the instruments that push things around down here. But in truth, it is a spiritual hierarchy that is executor of everything that gets done in the phenomenal universe.

For example, I am standing here at the podium at the head of the classroom. I am thirsty and would like a drink of water. I ask a student if he would be kind enough to bring me a glass of water. The kindly student gets up, goes to the water cooler at the back of the classroom, draws me a glass of water and delivers it to me.

This simple scenario doesn't seem very magical does it? However, from my point of view it was a miraculously successful conjuration. By strength of my will (and with only a few well-chosen magical words of enchantment) I set into obedient motion an entire hierarchy of spiritual beings;

- I, Rabbi Lamed Ben Clifford (the Deity),

- had a need which I defined and named as "thirst" (Divine Name of a desire formulated by the Deity—Atziluth).

- Activating my unambiguous spiritual authority as your teacher, I declare the Divine Name (vibrations of sound declaring my thirst) and inspire an archangel (student—Briah) to fulfill my desire.

- The archangel then activates an army of angels within himself (in Yetzirah); angels of the eye to seek out and locate the water cooler, angels of nerves and muscles and equilibrium to propel him through space and around obstacles until he reaches his goal.

- At the water cooler, the angel then employs the Intelligences and Spirits of gravity and hydrodynamics to fill the glass with water (Assiah).

- The process is then reversed until the archangel delivers the water to me thereby fulfilling the will of the Deity.

This may not be what you think of when you think of magick, but I assure you it is magick. In fact, most of the spiritual activity that took place in the above scenario actually occurred on the invisible plane. No one could see my words of enchantment. No one could see the internal processes that inspired and propelled the student to the water cooler, or the invisible force of gravity. For all intents and purposes, I wanted a drink of water and only seconds after focusing my will upon that desire, a glass of water traveled through space and appeared in my hands.

Since spirits do the dirty work of creation, Qabalistic magicians theorize that it is only logical that they should be compelled to work for us. After all, these guys are easily bamboozled. They go where they're pointed and do what they're told. They're accustomed to following orders from higher intelligences. However, in magick, it's not *what you know* but *who you are* that counts, and before you can proceed to bamboozle a spirit into believing you are a higher intelligence, you must first bamboozle *yourself* into believing you are a higher intelligence!

If I want to enchant Tina, the girl next door, to fall in love with me, it doesn't matter that I *know* that Jehovah Tzabaoth is that aspect of Deity served by Haniel, who governs Anael of the Elohim, who commands Hagiel by whom is Kedemel[2] compelled. I must first perfectly realize that somewhere in my own complex spiritual composition is a perfect working model of Jehovah Tzabaoth, Haniel, Elohim, Anael of the Elohim, Hagiel, and Kedemel. I must be able to actually identify with the top guy in my own organization, and from that position of authority *beseech* the archangel to help me *conjure* the angel that I may *order* the intelligence in his name so that the spirit will listen to me when I *command* it to do my bidding.

Now, does this mean that you will have to study and master all those tongue-twisting god-names and archangels, and angels that (let's face it) mean nothing to you? Does this mean that you will then have to labor to somehow integrate this mountain of memorized data into your subjective consciousness?

Hell no! You're a Chicken Qabalist! Don't worry about it! The essence of this wonderful organization is *already* integrated into your spiritual matrix. It (and the infinite number of other ways of looking at creation) came as standard equipment when you were born as a human being.

You can, of course, memorize all the goodies if you want to, and I'm sure there will be some of you who will want to.[3] But I want you to know that it is not essential to do so. It is only necessary that you program your spiritual worldview with this image of an ordered hierarchy of consciousness. Eventually, your recognition of these Qabalistic facts of life will enable you to effortlessly and naturally align and harmonize the various aspects of your consciousness *with* the Qabalistic facts of life. Once this is achieved (and it will most likely happen without you realizing that it *has* happened) you will discover *your* place in the divine hierarchy and why only you can fill that position.

I have prepared a flow chart (Table 3, pages 144–145) that shows the classic Qabalistic hierarchy of divine name, archangel, angel (and the angelic choir to which it belongs) and the intelligence and spirit attributed to each Sephirah on the Tree of Life. You can use this information to construct complex rituals of formal evocation, such as those found in any number of magical texts.

You can also design simple house-and-garden variety spells such as this ditty I wrote and recited at the appearance of Venus in the evening or early morning sky:

O Lord of Hosts, Jehovah Tzabaoth,
You know the dreams of fools.
Thee I invoke to hear my oath,
In Nogah where Venus rules.

O Haniel, Great Archangel.
Glory of God thou art,
Send Anael, love's bold Angel
To touch sweet Tina's heart.

Come Hagiel! Come Hagiel!
In Anael's name, obey!
Compel Kedemel to do my will.
Tina love me night and day!

Table 3. The Hierarchy of Spirits: Divine Name Governs Archangel who Governs Angel who Governs Intelligence who Governs Spirit.

SEPHIROTH of the Tree of Life	ATZILUTH Archetypal World — Divine Name	BRIAH Creative World — Archangel	YETZIRAH Formative World — Angel/Angelic Choir	ASSIAH Material World — Intelligence	Spirit
1. Kether Rashith ha-Gilgalim —Primum Mobile	Eheieh → *I Am*	Metatron → *Angel of the Presence*	Chayoth ha-Qadesh *(Holy Living Creatures)*	—	—
2. Chokmah Mazloth—the Zodiac	Yah → *God*	Raziel → *Secret of God*	Ophanim *(Wheels)*	—	—
3. Binah Shabbathai—Saturn	YHVH Elohim *Lord God*	Tzaphqiel → *Who covers God*	Cassiel → *of the Aralim (Mighty Ones)*	Agiel →	Zazel
4. Chesed Tzedek—Jupiter	El *God*	Tzadqiel → *Justice of God*	Sachiel → *of the Cashmalim (Brilliant Ones)*	Iophiel →	Hismael
5. Geburah Madim—Mars	Elohim Gibor *Almighty God*	Kamael → *Who sees God*	Zamael → *of the Seraphim (Flaming Serpents)*	Graphiel →	Bartzabel
6. Tiphareth Shemesh—Sol	YHVH Eloah va-Daath *Lord God of Knowledge*	Raphael → *God has healed*	Michael → *of the Melekim (Kings)*	Nakhiel →	Sorath
7. Netzach Nogah—Venus	YHVH Tzabaoth *Lord of Hosts*	Haniel → *Glory of God*	Anael → *of the Elohim (Gods)*	Hagiel →	Kedemel

Table 3. The Hierarchy of Spirits (cont.).

SEPHIROTH of the Tree of Life	ATZILUTH Archetypal World Divine Name	BRIAH Creative World Archangel	YETZIRAH Formative World Angel/Angelic Choir	ASSIAH Material World — Intelligence — Spirit
8. Hod Kokab—Mercury	Elohim Tzabaoth God of Hosts	→ Michael Who is as God	→ Raphael of the Beni Elohim (Sons of Gods)	Tiriel → Taphthartharath
9. Yesod Labanah—Luna	Shaddai El Chai Almighty Living God	→ Gabriel God is my strength	→ Gabriel (go figure) of the Kerubim (who intercede)	→ M.* → Chasmodai
10. Malkuth Olam Yesodoth Sphere of the Elements	Adonai ha-Aretz Lord of the Earth	→ Sandalphon Co-brother (tall Angel)	→ Eshim (Flames) ↓ ↓	

The Elemental World—Beneath the Angelic Choir of the Eshim, the Spirits of the four elements are divided into four categories, each governed by its own individual Elemental Divine Name, Archangel, Angel, Ruler, and King.

	Divine Name	Archangel	Angel	Ruler	King
Fire:	YHVH Tzabaoth	Michael	Aral	Seraph	Djin
Water:	Elohim	Gabriel	Taliahad	Tharsis	Nichsa
Air:	Shaddai El Chai	Raphael	Chassan	Ariel	Paralda
Earth:	Adonai ha-Aretz	Auriel	Phorlakh	Kerub	Ghob

*Intelligence of Yesod in Assiah: Malka be-Tarshishim ve-ad be-Ruah Shehaqim.

9

THE CHICKEN TAROT
AND
THE HOLY GUARDIAN ANGEL

Introduced by Lon Milo DuQuette

*The you that you think is you is not you. It is a dream you. In fact, the
you that you think is you is a dreamer inside a dreamer inside a
dreamer inside a dreamer. You are the King of the universe, who
has fallen asleep and is dreaming he is the Queen, who has fallen asleep
and is dreaming she is the Prince, who has fallen asleep
and is dreaming he is a sleeping Princess.*
—RABBI LAMED BEN CLIFFORD

Rabbi Ben Clifford's passionate embrace of the Tarot represents
perhaps his most dramatic departure from the traditions of
Orthodox Qabalah. His 1992 interview in the American Tarot journal, *Augury Today*, gave his enemies all the ammunition they would
need to permanently discredit him. Still, he seemed to enjoy the
ridicule heaped upon him from conservative quarters, and took
fiendish delight in promoting the study and use of the tarot cards.

While it is true that little or no evidence exists that would suggest that the Tarot was the invention of ancient Hebrew Qabalists, it
is obvious to anyone not blinded by sectarian prejudice that the 78

cards of a standard tarot deck are constructed, organized, and characterized in perfect harmony with fundamental Qabalistic principles.

It is a sad fact that Ben Clifford did not write extensively on the tarot. What follows is the entire *Augury Today* interview and illustrations reprinted with the kind permission of Credulity Publications, Inc. We must keep in mind the fact that in this interview Ben Clifford was addressing a readership of professional Tarot readers and enthusiasts, and not his own students (or imaginary students). Consequently, we see that he was obliged to introduce fundamental Qabalistic principals that have already been touched upon elsewhere in this book. I hope the reader will forgive these redundancies because the interview is a wonderful example of how the Rabbi went about introducing the Qabalah to non-Qabalists.

I should like especially to call the reader's attention to the final section of the interview in which Ben Clifford discusses the exceptional status of the four Princess cards of the tarot. Besides exhibiting the Rabbi at his irascible best, it is a marvelous essay that neatly dovetails many Qabalistic principles we've learned so far concerning the nature of the soul. It also introduces us to the concept of the Holy Guardian Angel, a key element of modern Qabalistic practices.

Long Island Queballa[1] Guru Sez Tarot Cards Are "Aleph-OK!"

BY IDA PENGALA

[AUGURY TODAY, VOL. II, NO. 2, JULY-AUGUST 1992. REPRINTED WITH
PERMISSION OF CREDULITY PUBLICATIONS, INC., CHICAGO]

AT: I'm talking today with Rabbi Lamed Ben Clifford. The Rabbi operates what I guess we could call an ashram at his home in Montauk, New York, where he teaches the marvelous-mystical-magical art of the Qabalah. Is that how you pronounce it Rabbi? Qabalah?

LBC: Pronounce it any damned way you want.

AT:: Well . . . so . . . I will then. Thank you. That lifts a burden from my shoulders. I'm always afraid I'm going to mispronounce all these exotic and esoteric words.

LBC: Lifting spiritual burdens is my job. I've worked hard to gain enlightenment just so you won't have to.

AT: Oh . . . well . . . Thank you. Now, Rabbi . . . may I call you Ben?

LBC: No.

AT: Right then. Let's start by asking why an authority on the Hebrew Qabalah such as yourself would be interested in Tarot cards?

LBC: Because working with the Tarot is the fastest way I know of learning Qabalistic fundamentals and one of the most practical things one can do with the Qabalah.

AT: I don't understand.

LBC: The Hebrew Qabalah forms the foundation of the Western Mystery Tradition and the Western Hermetic arts. This tradition includes Astrology, Alchemy, Jewish and Christian Mysticism, Ceremonial Magick, and Tarot. Of all of these disciplines, the Tarot is the most perfect representation of Qabalistic fundamentals and is the common denominator between the various systems.

Whether we realize it or not, when we work with the Tarot, we are working with the Qabalah. Tarot's like the DNA of the Qabalah—better than that—it's actually the picture-book of the Qabalah. I know there are many tarotists who are aware of the Qabalistic roots of the Tarot but, for one reason or another, they choose not to incorporate any Qabalistic wisdom in their arsenal of Tarot tools.

AT: Perhaps that's because the Qabalah is based on the Bible, is it not? How could it possibly be relevant to those of us who are not Jewish or Christian?

LBC: Some people think that because the Qabalah seems to be based on the Bible that it must be reserved for Jews or Christians, and therefore it has no place in neo-pagan or New Age thought. Such is not the case. The Qabalah is not a belief system. It's a way of looking at things. It's a way of organizing your universe so neatly that you eventually discover your own place in it. It's a way of connecting absolutely everything in the universe with absolutely everything else until, eventually, you achieve a transcendent level of consciousness in which you realize there is nothing left to connect.

AT: Is the Qabalah a book?

LBC: No, the Qabalah is not a book, but there are many Qabalistic texts, some of them are pretty bizarre. If you're not careful, you'll wind up squandering thirty or forty years of your life counting the nostril hairs of God. I know folks who have done just that. It's sad. It's worse than falling asleep with leprechauns when you're young, and waking up old and gray—with dead leaves in your pockets and snowflakes in your hair.

AT: Al . . . rrrighty then. Could you please explain your Qabalah universe and how it relates to the Tarot cards?

LBC: First of all, there is only one universe, only one absolute. Call it God. Call it what you want, but It's the One thing that contains all the other things in the world—It's the great One beyond which there is nothing. Now, that "nothing" is a pretty important concept in the Qabalah, because that's where the One and subsequently all the other stuff comes from. In the Tarot, this super-nothing is represented by the *Fool* card.

> *A pure buffoon skips toward his doom.*
>
> *An abyss of profound uncertainties.*
> *It takes a Fool to seed that womb*
> *With all possible, possibilities.*

Ultimately, the *Fool* is the only real Tarot card. In essence, all the other cards live inside the *Fool*—just like you and me and all the other components of creation live inside the inscrutable consciousness of Deity.

AT: Do all 78 cards live inside the *Fool* card?

LBC: Technically, yes. Of course they do. But for our purposes it will be better to think of the Tarot as two distinct groups of cards. The Greater Arcana (or the 22 Trumps); and the Lesser Arcana (56 cards broken up into four suits, each suit containing one Ace, four Court Cards, and nine Small Cards).

Let's look first at the trumps. We put the *Fool* under our microscope and we see that there are 22 trumps (including the *Fool*). These are the cards most people think of when they hear the word Tarot: *Fool, Magician, High Priestess, Empress, Emperor, Hierophant, Lovers, Chariot, Strength, Hermit, Wheel of Fortune, Justice, Hanged Man, Death, Temperance, Devil, Tower, Star, Moon, Sun, Judgement,* and *World.*

Now, there just so happens to be 22 letters in the Hebrew alphabet. What a coincidence! The Hebrew alphabet is really the foundation of the Qabalah and (though it might not be immediately obvious) the 22 trumps are the visual expressions of the 22 letters and their esoteric meanings.

Now, some of your readers, might use the 22 trumps exclusively when they read the cards for themselves or others. If that's the case, each spread could actually be spelling out words.

AT: You mean the cards could be literally spelling out the answer to a question?

LBC: That's exactly what I'm saying. Tell me, what is one of the most common questions a Tarot reader is asked to answer?

AT: Questions of romance, I suppose. "Should I marry my sweetheart?"

LBC: "Should I marry my sweetheart?" Fine! Using a standard ten-card Celtic-Cross spread with the *Empress* as the significator, you lay out the *Empress, Hierophant, Hanged Man, Tower, World, Emperor, High Priestess, Hermit, Sun* and *Justice.* I'm sure there are infinite ways to interpret these cards in this order, but one unmistakable characteristic of the spread is the fact that the cards spell the words "DUMP THE GIRL."

Vaporous mysticism is fine, but for Heaven's sake don't ignore the obvious! What if the *Hermit,* the *Magician* and the *Hanged Man* are really trying to tell your client to buy IBM?[2]

AT: My goodness! I had no idea . . .

LBC: I didn't think you did. Each of the 22 letters also has a basic meaning. For example, the Hebrew letter that is attributed to the *Fool* card is Aleph, and Aleph means "ox." Now, it's probably unlikely that any of your clients are ever going to scream, "My god, I'm going to marry an ox!" but there are many other relevant things to the modern world of which the word "ox" is suggestive—strength, stability, fertility, harnessed energy—see what I mean? You can never predict how your awareness of this attribute might someday trigger a psychic reaction and provide you and your client the answer.

The meanings of the Hebrew letters for the rest of the trumps are:

Magician—House

High Priestess—Camel or Rope

Empress—Door

Emperor—Window

Hierophant—Nail

Lovers—Sword

Chariot—Fence

Strength—Serpent

Hermit—Hand

Wheel of Fortune—Palm of the hand

Justice—Ox goad

Hanged Man—Water

Death—Fish

Temperance—Tent pole

Devil—Eye

Tower—Mouth

Star—Fish hook

Moon—Back of the head

Sun—Head or face

Judgement—Tooth

World—Mark or Signature or Cross

If you did nothing more than learn the meanings of the Hebrew letters for each trump you would have 22 additional sources of information to draw upon when reading the cards.

AT: Again, Rabbi, I have to say . . .

LBC: Look, do you want to hear what I have to say or not?

AT: Most certainly, I beg your . . .

LBC: Qabalists attribute twelve letters of the Hebrew alphabet to the signs of the zodiac, seven letters to the seven planets of the ancients, and three letters to the three primitive elements.

Now, it just so happens that the 22 trumps of the Tarot are divided and attributed in precisely the same way. What a coincidence! The *Emperor* is Aries, *Heirophant* Taurus, *Lovers* Gemini, *Chariot* Cancer, *Strength* Leo, *Hermit* Virgo, *Justice* Libra, *Death* Scorpio, *Temperance* Sagittarius, *Devil* Capricorn, *Star* Aquarius, and *Moon* Pisces.

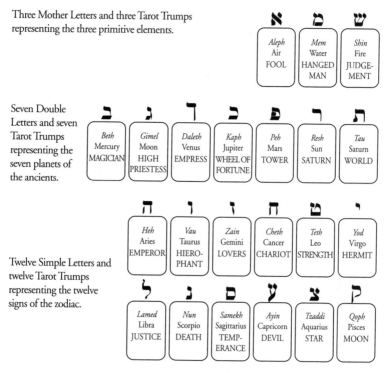

Three Mother Letters and three Tarot Trumps representing the three primitive elements.

| Aleph
Air
FOOL | Mem
Water
HANGED MAN | Shin
Fire
JUDGE-MENT |

Seven Double Letters and seven Tarot Trumps representing the seven planets of the ancients.

| Beth
Mercury
MAGICIAN | Gimel
Moon
HIGH PRIESTESS | Daleth
Venus
EMPRESS | Kaph
Jupiter
WHEEL OF FORTUNE | Peh
Mars
TOWER | Resh
Sun
SATURN | Tau
Saturn
WORLD |

Twelve Simple Letters and twelve Tarot Trumps representing the twelve signs of the zodiac.

| Heh
Aries
EMPEROR | Vau
Taurus
HIERO-PHANT | Zain
Gemini
LOVERS | Cheth
Cancer
CHARIOT | Teth
Leo
STRENGTH | Yod
Virgo
HERMIT |
| Lamed
Libra
JUSTICE | Nun
Scorpio
DEATH | Samekh
Sagittarius
TEMP-ERANCE | Ayin
Capricorn
DEVIL | Tzaddi
Aquarius
STAR | Qoph
Pisces
MOON |

Figure 29. The 22 tarot trumps are created by the 22 letters of the sacred Hebrew alphabet.

In a reading, a zodiacal trump might obviously be pointing to a specific time of year, perhaps the questioner's birth-sign, or that of someone else important to the reading. Maybe the card is pinpointing an appropriate time to schedule an event such as a wedding, or a vacation.

AT: But aren't these attributes astrological rather than Qabalistic?

LBC: Hello? Don't you get it? Astrology and Qabalah come from the same place. Duh! Now please, let me go on.

Signs of the zodiac represent more than just time coordinates. Each sign (and consequently each zodiac trump) has attached to it a litany of traditional plants, animals, precious stones, foods, drugs, and deities sacred to cultures and mythologies from around the world. All these attributes are hiding just below the surface of each card. I've got them all organized in a giant Rolodex in my garage.

Whether we consciously recognize them or not, these are archetypal images that we share with every other human being on the planet—and Qabalah is the glue that holds them all together. Depending upon the circumstances, the *Justice* card could stand for an emerald, or an aloe plant, or an elephant. The *Emperor* might suggest ruby, or geranium, or a ram.

AT: But how can a tarot reader apply this information practically in a reading?

LBC: It all depends upon the question. If it concerns matters of health, a zodiac sign is attributed to each part of the body. The *Moon* card (Pisces) could indicate the feet, or the *Lovers* (Gemini), the lungs, or *Strength* card (Leo), the heart. There's no end to the applications.

Now please, I would like to move on to the planetary trumps. I'm getting hungry. You *did* say the magazine was treating me to dinner, didn't you?

AT: Yes, of course, the Carnegie Deli if you like.

LBC: Dear God no! Maybe Ethiopian food.

AT: Whatever you would like. You were going to tell us about planetary trumps.

LBC: I love Ethiopian food.

AT: Ethiopian food then.

LBC: Great! Okay let's look at planetary trumps: The *Magician* is Mercury, the *High Priestess* is Luna, the *Empress* is Venus, the *Wheel of Fortune* is Jupiter, the *Tower* is Mars, the *Sun* card is the Sun, and the *World* is Saturn.

Those of your readers who are familiar with astrology know how important planetary influences are to a person's life. Obviously, we're not all astrologers, but the planetary trumps (like the zodiac trumps) have lots of traditional correspondences based on the Qabalah. For instance, each of the seven planets represents a day of the week. The *Sun* card obviously represents Sunday, the *High Priestess* is the Moon and Monday, the *Tower* is Mars and Tuesday, the *Magician* is Mercury and Wednesday, the *Wheel of Fortune* is Jupiter and Thursday, the *Empress* is Venus and Friday, the *World* is Saturn and Saturday.

Each of the planetary trumps also can point to one of the planetary metals. You may not think you will ever need to use this information in a reading, but just in case, it might be helpful to know that mercury is the metal for the *Magician*, silver rules the *High Priestess*, copper rules the *Empress*, tin rules the *Wheel of Fortune*, iron rules the *Tower*, gold rules the *Sun*, and lead rules the *World*.

The planetary trumps also represent parts of the human body. This information could be helpful in a reading concerning health matters. The *Magician* rules the nervous system, the *High Priestess* the lymphatic system, the *Empress* rules the reproductive system, the *Wheel of Fortune* rules the digestive system, the *Tower* rules the muscles, the *Sun* rules the circulatory system, and the *World* card rules the bones.

AT: That leaves three final trump cards which stand for the elements—Air, Water, and Fire—Am I correct?

LBC: Correct.

AT: What happened to the Earth element? Is there no room for Earth in your Qabalah universe?

LBC: Don't be absurd. Of course there is room for Earth. But Earth is somewhat the stepchild of the universe—in precisely the same way that human beings are somewhat the stepchildren in the family of spiritual beings. We're vitally important stepchildren, however, and I want to talk about that later. But now let's get back to the elemental trumps.

There are three (actually four) trumps that represent elements: The *Fool* represents Air, the *Hanged Man* Water, and *Judgement*, Fire. These three trumps are attributed to the three Mother Letters of the Hebrew alphabet, Aleph, Mem, and Shin. The fourth element—Earth—is represented by the *World* card that assumes double duty with the very compatible planet Saturn.

From a Qabalist's point of view, the elements (as represented by the four elemental trumps) convey a much higher octave of significance than the elemental building-blocks of nature which we will soon see are represented by the Aces, Court Cards and Small Cards. The elemental trumps might be more accurately viewed as profound and primitive spiritual elements.

For instance, the Air of the *Fool*, instead of representing the mundane concepts of Air, symbolizes the vital essence that animates all life (the Breath of Life). The Water of the *Hanged Man* is the Great Sea—the universal menstrum that carries the vital essence of life (the Blood of Life); the Fire of *Judgement* is the central fire of life—the Holy Spirit—the spark that sustains, and finally consumes and transforms all existence.

The *World*, being last and lowest of the trumps, represents both the planet Saturn and the element Earth. Saturn, according to mythology, swallowed his own children. This dual attribution is a not so subtle hint that Earth is both the end and the beginning—the foundation of the universe and its dissolution.

However, some very basic and practical attributes of the four elemental trumps are particularly helpful to me when I read the cards. For instance, they can be used to determine direction. The *Fool* is Air, which by tradition indicates the East; the *Hanged Man* is Water and the West; *Judgement* is Fire, traditionally sacred to the South; and the *World* is Earth, symbolic of the cold North. I'm sure your readers can imagine a circumstance where this directional information could be helpful in a reading?

Finally (and then we're going to move on to the Lesser Arcana—I'm starving to death), the four elemental trumps can represent our senses: The *Fool* smells . . .

AT: (Laughter)

LBC: Oh grow up! The *Hanged Man* tastes, *Judgement* sees, and the *World* touches and feels.

AT: Rabbi, I must tell you that I have learned more practical information in just these few minutes than I have in nearly ten years of working with the tarot cards. Are all Qabalists tarot experts also?

LBC: I'm sad to say that most traditional Kabbalists (they spell it with a K and two Bs) accuse me of apostasy. They hold me and my teachings in great contempt. They view my practical applications of the tarot as unspiritual and my embrace of universal religious concepts as very heretical. But I don't care. I tell my students if they don't intend to actually use this information for their own spiritual enlightenment then get out. I call my brand of Qabalah *Chicken Qabalah* to show that I'm proud to be a practical holy man.

AT: You seem to be just that, Rabbi. Now, please tell us about the Lesser Arcana—the Aces, the Court Cards, and the Small Cards.

LBC: Okay—the trumps are what we saw when we sliced the

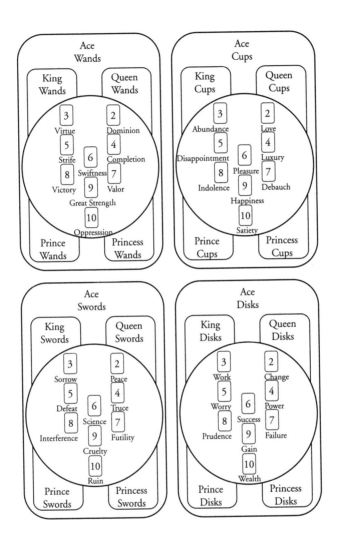

Figure 30. The Aces hold the Court Cards and the Small Cards.

FOOL into 22 pieces. But if we slice the *Fool* into only four pieces we see the four Aces—and inside each Ace we find four Court Cards, and nine Small Cards. Can you visualize that?

AT: But why four? Why are there four Aces? Why are there four suits in the tarot?

LBC: That is the best question you've asked today. Most of us are aware that the four suits are by tradition attributed to the elements of Fire, Water, Air, and Earth. But where did the concept of these four elements come from? The answer comes straight out of the most fundamental doctrine of Hebrew mysticism—the Great Four-Letter Name of God—YOD HEH VAU HEH. Most nonJews pronounce this Jehovah. Most Jews hold the word in such reverence they never pronounce it at all. Hermetic Qabalists refer to it by its technical name, Tetragrammaton.

In Hebrew mysticism and Qabalah, the great absolute Deity is too abstract to think about. I guess they figured they had a better chance at conceptualizing Deity if they chopped It up into pieces and then methodically meditated about the pieces. The Number Two was still too abstract, and the Number Three was held in such veneration that I guess they finally decided that it would be okay to chop Deity up into four pieces that they called Yod Heh Vau Heh.

To these four pieces they attributed four worlds, which are really layers or frequencies of divine consciousness by which Deity creates everything with Its own thought.

AT: How does that work exactly?

LBC: How does that work exactly? Give me a break here! If I knew how it worked—exactly—I would be as smart as the Deity, wouldn't I? Theoretically, here's the drill: the Deity gets a good idea up in world number 1 (Atziluth, the Archetypal World); and then that idea gets organized in world number 2 (Briah, the Creative World); then that organized idea gets visualized and formulated into a blueprint of the idea in world number 3 (Yetzirah, the Formative World); and finally, the idea actually manifests as an object, or a force, or an energy, down here in world number 4 (Assiah, the Material World). The concept is sort of like the Will, the Heart, the Mind, and the Flesh of Deity.

Because, according to Qabalistic tradition, each of us was created in the image of this four-part Deity, each of our souls is also divided up into four parts. The highest part of the soul is called the Chiah, the Life-Force itself. Then comes the Neshamah (the Soul Intuition), then the Ruach (our Intellect), and finally, the Nephesh (our Animal Soul). The four suits of the tarot are a perfect reflection of this concept. Can you see this?

AT: I think so. I can picture the Deity divided into four parts, and I can imagine the same with the soul, but I don't quite understand exactly how the four parts of Deity and the four parts of our souls are connected.

LBC: Just pretend the Deity is comprised of four incredibly gigantic tuning forks that are vibrating four musical notes in a descending scale. (Remember these are vibrations of consciousness, not sound.) Now pretend your soul is comprised of four tiny tuning forks tuned to the same four notes. Even though our tuning forks are infinitely smaller, they are still set into motion by the vibrations of the Deity's tuning forks, and vibrate in perfect tandem with them. Do you follow me?

AT: Yes, I believe so.

LBC: If you divide the 56 cards of the Lesser Arcana into four stacks, one for Wands, Cups, Swords, and Disks, you have this fourfold universe laid out in front of you. To really organize your world, lay each of the four stacks face up, with the Ace on top. Beneath the Ace put the four Court Cards (King, Queen, Prince, Princess), then the Small Cards (2 through 10).

The four stacks with the Aces on top are the four letters in the Great Name, YOD HEH VAU HEH, and the cards underneath are the pieces of Deity, Its universe and our own souls. The Wands are the Yod stack, and by tradition are attributed to Fire; the Cups live in the first Heh stack and represent the Water element; the Swords are the Vau stack and Air; and the Disks are the Final Heh stack and are attributed to the Earth element.

162 / C H I C K E N Q A B A L A H

Now these elements are more than just the fire in your fireplace, or the water in your swimming pool, or the air in your lungs, or the earth in your garden. They are all things—all forces—all energies in the universe divided into categories that are either fiery in nature (like nuclear radiation, or Tabasco sauce, or enthusiasm); or watery in nature (like electromagnetism, or beer, or mirrors); or airy in nature (like daydreams, or radio signals, or winds) or earthy in nature (like a coal mine, or stubbornness, or gravity).

It's the job of these four elements to join with other elements in different combinations and proportions to create the universe. They do this with the help of a fifth element called Spirit. Spirit enables the elements to stick together the same way atoms bond together to form molecules. At the same time, this magical element, Spirit, serves to separate the individual elements just enough so that each tiny unit of Fire, or Water, or Air, or Earth maintains its elemental identity. If Spirit didn't exist, the four elements would just smash together, turning the universe into mush.

Spirit is represented in both the Greater and Lesser Arcana of the Tarot. The *Judgement* card, as we recall, does double-duty as the Trump that represents both Spirit and Fire. But it is in the Lesser Arcana that Spirit reveals itself in remarkable detail by the four Aces, the Court Cards, and the Small Cards that live inside them (see figure 30, page 159).

The four Aces are really the big YOD, HEH, VAU, HEH and everything that goes with it. The *Ace of Wands* is Spirit of Fire; *Ace of Cups* is Spirit of Water; *Ace of Swords* is Spirit of Air; *Ace of Disks* is Spirit of Earth.

Together, the four Court Cards of each suit are a miniature YOD HEH VAU HEH that subdivides their Aces into four parts. Kings are the fiery nature of their suit, Queens are the watery nature of their suit, Princes are the airy nature of their suit, and the Princesses are the earthy nature of their suit. Are you following this?

The *King of Wands* is Fire of Fire. Do you see? Fire because he is a King, and Fire because he's a Wand. The *King of Cups* would be Fire of Water. Fire because he is King, and Water because his suit is Cups. See how it goes? The *Queen of Cups* would be . . . ?

AT: Water of Water!

LBC: and the *Princess of Swords* would be . . . ?

AT: Earth of Air—the Princess is the *earthy* nature of her suit and Swords are Air. I get it!

LBC: The Qabalist sees the wonders of creation as the result of the Deity shuffling the cards and dealing them out in different numbers and combinations. It shuffles and draws three or four here—perhaps to create the elemental recipe for a duck; or it deals out three or four cards over there to create pond scum or an aardvark. Do you see what I'm saying?

AT: Yes! Absolutely fascinating! But how can we use this information to help us out in a tarot reading? Court Cards are for me the most difficult cards to interpret.

LBC: With the Court Cards, we are in luck, because the Kings, Queens, and Princes each represent 30 degrees of the year (from 20° of one zodiac sign to 20° of the next sign).

AT: What about the Princesses?

LBC: Good question. I'll talk about the Princesses later. For the time being, let's just look at the Kings, Queens, and Princes. The reason why these twelve Court Cards rule from 20° of one sign to 20° of the next is to underscore the necessity for the elements to mix with other elements. If they ruled the entire 30° of a zodiac sign there would be no elemental mix. Besides, we already have twelve perfectly good zodiacal cards represented by the twelve zodiac trumps.

It's pretty easy to determine which days in any given year a King, Queen, or Prince represents. This is extremely helpful in a reading, especially when inspiration fails us. At such times we can always remember that the *Queen of Cups* represents June 11th to July 11th, or the *Knight of Disks* is August 12th to September 11th.[3] This is also helpful knowledge if you wanted to use a person's birthdate as a significator, or it might even be the birth card of someone who is important to the reading.

It can be even more meaningful to think about the elemental mix of a Court Card, and how that would translate in the character of an individual or a situation. Kings are the fiery aspect of their suit and so display the most violent and dynamic aspects of their element, also the most fleeting. Queens, being watery, are receptive and hold on to, as well as reflect, the nature of their suit (although, like a good mother, she will eventually relinquish her hold to pass it on to her children). The Prince and Princess are literally the offspring of the King and Queen; the Prince the more active of the two.

Certain elements combine harmoniously and others don't, but don't think you can nail down hard and fast definitions to the character of any tarot card by simply combining buzzwords. No card lives in a vacuum. Its ultimate meaning depends on its relation to its neighbors and the nature of the question. For this reason, the tarot reader should ideally be a Qabalist—armed with the knowledge of the fundamental classifications of everything in his or her universe. Eventually illumination will come, not through analysis or contemplation, but as the result of profound and simple observation.

AT: Why Rabbi, that's sublime. I hardly know what to say.

LBC: Good. Now let's talk about the 36 Small Cards. (I won't forget the Princesses). Each of the 36 Small Cards represents one decan (10°) of the year. Their positions are determined with perfect Qabalistic logic, and they nestle neatly under the rulership of a King, or a Queen, or a Prince of their suit. I brought a couple of charts that I hope you can print with this interview to show this far better than I can explain it.

Each of the 36 Small Cards (in figure 31, page 165) represents one decan (10°) of the zodiac:

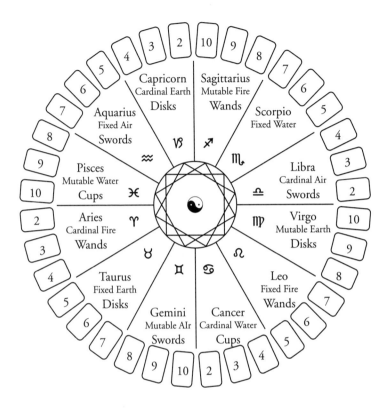

Figure 31. Each of the 36 Small Cards rules one decan (10°) of the Zodiac.

◆ The 2s, 3s, 4s represent the *cardinal* signs of the zodiac: Aries, Cancer, Libra, and Capricorn;

◆ The 5s, 6s, 7s represent the *fixed* signs of the zodiac: Taurus, Leo, Scorpio, and Aquarius;

◆ The 8s, 9s, 10s represent the *mutable* signs of the zodiac: Gemini, Virgo, Sagittarius, and Pisces.

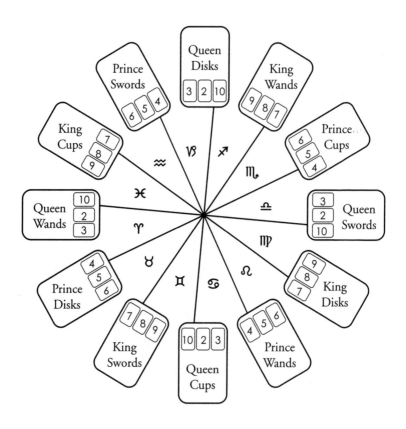

Figure 32. Rulership of the Kings, Queens, and Princes. It is the cosmic duty of the elements to mix with each other and knit creation together. Therefore, instead of ruling from 0° to 0° of each zodiac sign, the Kings, Queens, and Princes rule from 20° of one sign to 20° of the next.

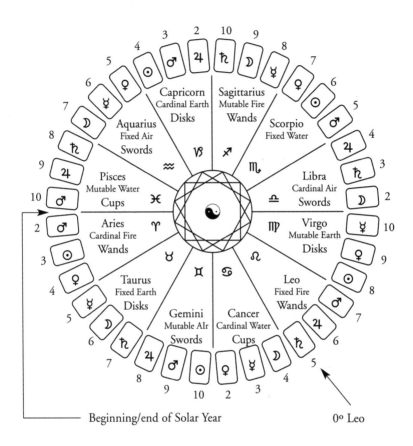

Figure 33. The planets allotted to the Small Cards on the Tree of Life. Starting with 0° Leo, the planets are in descending order: Saturn (♄), Jupiter (♃), Mars (♂), Sun (☉), Venus (♀), Mercury (☿), Moon (☽). Mars is repeated at the end and beginning of the solar year.

In other words, the 2, 3, and 4 of Wands represent the 1st, 2nd and 3rd decan of Aries—because 2s, 3s and 4s represent Cardinal Signs. Wands are Fire and Aries is the cardinal fire sign of the zodiac.

AT: As simple as that?

LBC: As simple as that. And not only that, a planet is also assigned to each of the 36 Small Cards. Starting with 0º Leo (the *5 of Wands*), planets are allotted to the Small Cards in descending Tree of Life order. For your readers who are unfamiliar with the Tree of Life, I'll just tell you what that order is: Saturn, Jupiter, Mars, Sun, Venus, Mercury, Moon.

You'll notice that Mars repeats itself at the last decan of Pisces and the first decan of Aries. Qabalists explain this by saying that at the end of winter and the beginning of spring the year needs an extra boost of Mars' strength to help usher in spring. (Hey! Don't blame me. I didn't invent the system.)

Now can you see where the Small Cards get their traditional meanings? It's a combination of their Qabalistic and astrological attributes. The *2 of Wands* is called *Dominion* because it is first and foremost a strong and fiery Wand, the suit of the Will; then it is a Two, the purest and strongest position in the Small Card sequence; then it is the first decan of Aries, the strong, aggressive and energy-filled sign of the zodiac; finally, the planet attributed to the *2 of Wands* is Mars, and Mars is very, very happy to be in Aries. In other words—Wand plus Two plus Aries plus Mars equals "*Dominion.*"

All the Small Cards aren't as obvious as the *2 of Wands*, but I guarantee that if you carefully examine the suit, the number, the zodiac sign, and the planet attributed to each Small Card, you will eventually see why it bears its traditional meaning—why the *3 of Cups* is *Love*, why the *6 of Wands* is *Victory*, and the *9 of Swords* is *Despair* and *Cruelty*.

AT: Absolutely amazing. I guess I always thought the traditional titles were . . . well . . . traditional.

LBC: Traditionally Qabalistic. Okay, I want to wind this interview up. I'm really hungry! I promised to talk about the four Princesses. These four maids are treated differently from the other twelve Court Cards. This stems from the Qabalistic doctrine concerning the *exiled* condition of the human soul.

Now, when I say "exiled" I'm not referring to the old superstition about Adam and Eve getting kicked out of the Garden of Eden, and now we're all under some kind of bad *ju-ju* from an abusive creator. And I'm certainly not talking about that obscene and perverted doctrine known as *original sin*. Whoever the ignorant, woman-hating, insecure, irrational, terrified, guilt-ridden, diabolical, self-despising horse's ass was who came up with that diseased and malevolent concept should have been thrown into the Nebuchadnezzar Institute for the Criminally Insane. The ridiculous belief that humanity could be cursed and condemned to eternal torment because mythological characters fiddled with the wrong fruit has caused more suffering and mental illness than any other "religious" or political concept in history (coughing).

It still amazes me that seemingly normal people—folks with pagers and computers—folks who can fill out their own tax forms and program their VCRs, can walk around and smile with this malignant spiritual tumor nestled deep within their otherwise intelligent brains. It's not only absurd, it's downright toxic!

The story of Adam and Eve was originally written as a Qabalistic fable. It, and many of the other "Holy Scriptures," were crafted to illustrate profound cosmological and spiritual principles. They were created by and for very smart and highly educated specialists in the field of spiritual literature. They are technical texts that were never intended to be consumed like horror comics, and then misinterpreted to further the ambitions of mean-spirited religious bullies (coughing) and others who just can't seem to (coughing) resist the temptation to enslave the minds and the *sex-lives* of their fellow creatures (coughing).

AT: Rabbi, can I get you a glass of water?

LBC: Thank you, please. It just gets me so mad. Sorry. Where were we?

AT: We were talking about the Princesses.

LBC: Right! Remember what I said about four suits representing the four Qabalistic worlds, and that the human soul is a microcosmic reflection of this gigantic four-part reality?

AT: Yes, and that the four Court Cards in each suit are further subdivisions of all this . . .

LBC: Correct. Now think about the Court Card Kings as representing Atziluth (the Archetypal World), and, at the same time representing the highest part of each of our souls, the Chiah (the Life-Force);

AT: Okay.

LBC: Queens represent the second highest world, Briah (the Creative World), and our Neshamah (the Soul Intuition). Princes represent Yetzirah (the Formative World), and the Ruach, our Intellect; and finally, Princesses represent the lowest world, Assiah (the Material World) and the lowest part of our soul, the Nephesh (the Animal Soul). Follow me?

AT: Why yes. Amazingly enough, I believe I do.

LBC: Okay . . . listen up. Assiah, the material world we see around us, is just the lowest vibratory expression of the universe. It is where the pure consciousness of Deity is so slowed down—so doped up—that it actually crystallizes. It is where light and energy become matter and the invisible becomes visible.

The Nephesh, the Animal Soul, is our own personal version of Assiah. It is the only world our Nephesh recognizes. From this extremely limited point of view, both Deity and you and me are trapped, exiled in a frozen prison of matter. We are a Princess who has forgotten her royal birthright. We have fooled ourselves into believing that Assiah is the only reality. We identify ourselves completely with this lowest level of divine consciousness and the lowest part of our soul. But there is a way out—a way to escape the prison of matter and live in the bliss of the highest Qabalistic world. A classic fairytale shows us the way.

A Princess, a daughter of a King and Queen, is the victim of a magic spell and falls into a deep coma. A charming Prince (also the son of a King and Queen) sees the motionless perfection of this sleeping beauty and falls hopelessly in love with her image. Even though she is asleep (and unlikely to respond in kind) the Prince stoops down into her sarcophagus and kisses her. The pure love coursing through his lips is the magic that awakens the Princess. She is lifted from her tomb and marries the Prince, the act of which simultaneously makes her the Queen and him the King.

That's where the fairytale stops, but in the Qabalah, the new King then makes his new Queen pregnant. After doing this, he rolls over and goes to sleep. The Queen gives birth to twins, a Prince and a Princess, who leave the castle for adventures of their own. They get separated. She gets cursed—falls asleep—yada yada yada—we know the story from there.

That's how Kings are made. If there were no Princesses—there could be no Kings. She may be asleep, she may be slumbering in the deepest forest, guarded by height-challenged mining engineers, but without her redemption the old sleeping King will never reawaken, and the entire electricity of the universe will short-circuit. This two-way incestuous circuitry is the dynamo that creates and sustains the universe.

AT: This is all very quaint, Rabbi, but how does it apply to . . .

LBC: We're talking about you and me here, booby. The you that you think is you is not you. It is a dream you. In fact, the you that you think is you is a dreamer inside a dreamer inside a dreamer inside a dreamer. You are the King of the universe, who has fallen asleep and is dreaming he is the Queen, who has fallen asleep and is dreaming she is the Prince, who has fallen asleep and is dreaming he is a sleeping Princess.

The first step in our return to our original state is to trick our own Prince into kissing us and waking us up. This is pretty difficult, but it's not impossible, because we've all got one of these Princes running around in the "more awake" world. Even now, he's beating his fists against the lid of our glass coffin, trying to wake us up so he can marry us and can get on with his career. Modern Qabalistic magicians call this Prince the Holy Guardian Angel and view the union with their HGA as the first step toward spiritual enlightenment.

AT: How do we achieve union with our Holy Guardian Angel?

LBC: You do it by falling head-over-heels in love with love. You do it by using your inner imagination to create the Deity in the image of your most ideal lover, and then surrendering yourself completely and unconditionally.

Now this may sound uncomfortably like what Christians, and Buddhists, and Hindus tell you that you must do to their guys, and up to a point it is. But, no matter what they may tell you, no religion or creed can corner the market on this universal experience. It is totally universal and nonsectarian. It really doesn't matter what you call the object of your devotion, or how you visualize it. Anything and everything is capable of being the focus for your love for the Holy Guardian Angel.

Now can you see why the Princesses are special? Like you and me, they are positioned at the lowest end of the elemental universe, but they also embody the foundation of the entire universe, and are the key ingredient in the great recipe of creation.

Qabalists call the dream world of the sleeping Princess the *Microcosm*, or little universe. It is the world of Assiah and the Nephesh part of our soul. They place it at the very bottom on the Tree of Life. Here, I have some illustrations.

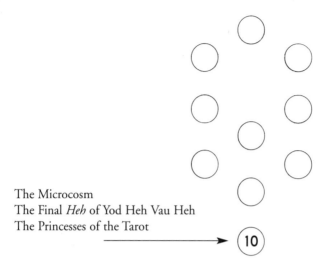

The Microcosm
The Final *Heh* of Yod Heh Vau Heh
The Princesses of the Tarot

Figure 34. The World of the Princesses.

The world of the Prince is Yetzirah, the next higher Qabalistic world, which is known as the *Macrocosm*, the big world. In us it's our Ruach. On the Tree of Life, the Macrocosm is attributed to the six Sephiroth in the middle of the Tree.

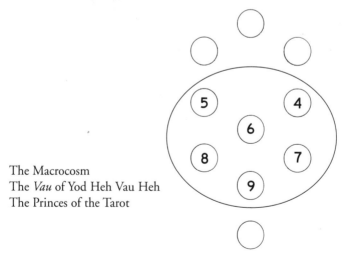

The Macrocosm
The *Vau* of Yod Heh Vau Heh
The Princes of the Tarot

Figure 35. The World of the Princes.

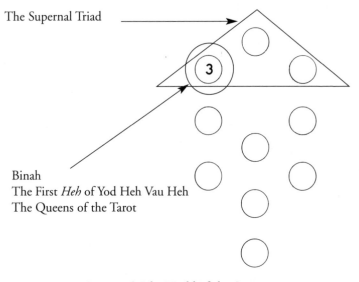

The Supernal Triad

Binah
The First *Heh* of Yod Heh Vau Heh
The Queens of the Tarot

Figure 36. The World of the Queens.

The world of the Queen is Briah, the next higher Qabalistic world, which is represented on the Tree of Life by the third Sephirah of the Supernal Triad, Binah. This corresponds to the Neshamah part of our soul, the Soul Intuition.

The world of the King is Atziluth, the highest Qabalistic world, which is represented on the Tree of Life by the first and second Sephiroth of the Supernal Triad, Kether and Chokmah, and the Chiah part of our soul, the Life-Force, itself.

AT: This is all breathtakingly interesting Rabbi. I can see why the Princesses and the Earth element are unique and important, and I certainly do want to hear more about this Holy Guardian Angel fellow, but before we end our interview you promised to explain why the Princesses do not represent degrees of the zodiac like the other twelve Court Cards.

LBC: You're right. I have rambled on, haven't I? Well, I had to, in order for you to see that the Princesses are just as much a defining

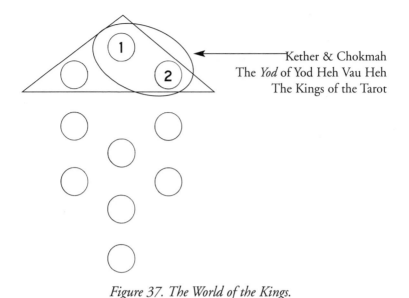

Kether & Chokmah
The *Yod* of Yod Heh Vau Heh
The Kings of the Tarot

Figure 37. The World of the Kings.

key to their suit as the Ace is. The Ace and the Princess are like the Alpha and Omega of their suit. Actually the Princess is the Throne of her Ace.

While the other Court Cards and Small Cards represent coordinates of time, by ruling degrees of the zodiac and days of the year, the Aces and their Princesses rule quadrants of Heaven which translate to quadrants of space and areas right here on Earth.

Imagine yourself looking down upon the North Pole of the Earth. Now divide the world in two by drawing a line that runs from the North Pole through Giza and all the way around the world back to the North Pole. Then quarter section the globe by drawing another line at a right angle to the first. The four quadrants of Earth are attributed in Yod Heh Vau Heh order thusly:

♦   The Quadrant east of Giza or most of Asia is ruled by the Ace and Princess of Wands;

♦   The Ace and Princess of Cups rule the area of the Pacific;

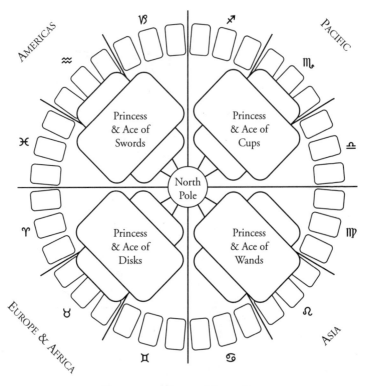

Figure 38. The world coordinates.

- ◆ The Ace and Princess of Swords rule the Americas; and

- ◆ The Ace and Princess of Disks rule most of Europe and Africa. (See figure 38.)

AT: This is incredible information. It could be very helpful in readings concerning global matters or international finance.

LBC: Or if the question treats on the subject of travel.

AT: Absolutely amazing.

LBC: You know, just winding up here, you and your readers might not think that learning all these attributes is going to help your Tarot readings in any way, and I can't promise that it will. But what I can promise is that in the process of learning these traditional attributes, you'll discover that you're giving yourself a wonderful liberal arts education in religion and philosophy.

It's possible that you might never be called upon to use any of this Qabalistic information in your career as a Tarot reader. But, I can almost guarantee that, as a result of your study, you'll discover that you've become a more interesting and eloquent person. And these are certainly traits people look for in a competent reader of Tarot.

AT: Rabbi Lamed Ben Clifford, it has indeed been a pleasure and a most enlightening afternoon. Thank you very much. I'm sure our readers will find this most provocative.

10

RABBI LAMED BEN CLIFFORD'S LAST LECTURE: GAMES QABALISTS PLAY

Introduced by Lon Milo DuQuette

In the game of Qabalah the object of the play is to lose yourself—the winner gets nothing, and you've only yourself to play with.
—RABBI LAMED BEN CLIFFORD

This chapter is perhaps the most unusual in the entire book. It was compiled from fragmentary notes and diagrams that represent, as far as I can determine, the last known instructional writings of Rabbi Lamed Ben Clifford. Less than three weeks after he scribbled the following apparently unfinished essay, he was reported missing by his disciples. The police found nothing in his apartment that would indicate foul play, or give them any clue as to the circumstances of his disappearance. A search of local newspaper clippings of that period revealed nothing out of the ordinary occurring that week in his Montauk neighborhood, other than a brief electrical brownout and an unseasonably intense infestation of gnats.

Personally, I would like to believe that the man who called himself Rabbi Lamed Ben Clifford is still alive and living somewhere on the East Coast. His work now done, he has dropped his colorful persona and resumed whatever life he had before his bizarre incarnation as the rebel Rabbi and guru of the Chicken Qabalah movement.

This last paper appears to be yet another address to the imaginary students of Z.I.P.Y., serving as their introduction to the fundamentals of Gematria, Notariqon, and Temura. But as we will see, the essay repeatedly dissolves into the most extraordinary digressions, and becomes something quite more.

This work ends abruptly with a curious poignant musing on the perfection of the universe. It is clear by the tone and intensity of the "lecture" up until that point that Ben Clifford was approaching the transcendent level of consciousness he so often advertised possible through the practice of Qabalistic exercises—a state of mind in which he perceived virtually everything connected, reflected, and forming the pattern for everything else.

We feel an almost voyeuristic self-consciousness as we peer through the window of his words, to glimpse the fabled Qabalistic chain-reaction of thoughts coursing like a multiple helix through his remarkable mind. "What does it all mean?" he asks repeatedly. "Who cares!" he joyfully answers, with Zen-like nonattachment. Whether it is madness or illumination, we can't help but stand in mute admiration, as he valiantly struggles to keep objectively focused on the subject at hand. Again and again he loses the fight, and merrily slips the bonds of linear rationality, plunging deep into the heart of the very processes he is trying to describe. In so doing, he demonstrates that the soul of the Qabalah is truly universal, revealing itself not only in Hebrew letters and books of the Bible, but in things as familiar as one's own name, or as innocuous as the words, "Have a nice day!"

Gematria, Notariqon, Temura—
Games Qabalists Play

NOTES TOWARD AN ADDRESS BY
RABBI LAMED BEN CLIFFORD*
TO THE GRADUATING STUDENTS OF THE
ZERUBBABEL INSTITUTE OF PHILOSOPHICAL YOUTH

I'VE TITLED TODAY'S TALK "Gematria, Notariqon and Temura—Games Qabalists Play." I can tell by the looks on your guileless faces that you have been looking forward to this discourse. After all, isn't this what most of you think Qabalah is all about—playing games with numbers, and letters, and words, until you decipher a personal message from God explaining the secrets of creation and affirming the fact that you are the Holy Chosen One? Well, my hapless hatchlings, by playing these games you can, indeed, discover the secrets of creation. You may even become afflicted with the knowledge that you are, in fact, the Holy Chosen One. (For God's sake—please don't tell anybody!) But I think that it's only fair to warn you that Qabalistic games are very powerful, and different from any other games you have ever played.

First of all we need to know why we are encouraged to play these mind-bending games. Let's start by reviewing what we've learned from the Ten Command-Rants:

1. All is One.

Realization of the "One" is the second-to-last goal of all Qabalists.

2. The First Command-Rant is a lie—All is Nothing.

The final goal is to attain consciousness of Nothing.

3. There really isn't a creation, time, or space, Heaven, or Earth . . . but there is a you!

Aren't you happy to hear that?

4. We perceive there is a creation, time, and space, Heaven, and Earth because of a fundamental defect in our powers of perception.

Our faulty powers of perception keep us trapped in illusionary existence.

5. This defect cannot be repaired, but it can be overcome.

How do we overcome this defect?

6. In order to overcome our defective powers of perception, we must be willing to abuse them until they break.

Bingo! But this can be very dangerous. It may be true that every enlightened sage is insane, but it does not necessarily follow that every insane person is an enlightened sage! We must employ discipline, and strictly limit our techniques of self-abuse to fundamental observations of the illusionary world around us. These observations reveal to us that:

7. Everything in Heaven and Earth is connected to everything in Heaven and Earth.

8. Everything in Heaven and Earth is the reflection of everything in Heaven and Earth.

9. Everything in Heaven and Earth contains the pattern of everything in Heaven and Earth.

You are not likely to gain enlightenment simply by examining all the "things" in illusionary Heaven and Earth. But it is possible to achieve realization of the One (the second-to-last goal of all Qabalists) by a profound and transcendent awareness that you are an indispensable component of the connections, the reflections, and the patterns of the Supreme Being.

10. Look hard enough at anything and you will eventually see everything.

The object of your observation can be anything at all. Qabalists have learned, however, that some things reveal the Divine connection-reflection-pattern easier than others.

Mathematics is the most profound example because it lays bare, to the tenacious student, the very structure of the universe. Language is another excellent tool for spiritual dissection because, by its very nature, it is a vehicle of connections, reflections, and patterns. Language evokes and transfers images from mind to mind in a manner not dissimilar to the creative fiat of the mythological gods of creation.

• • •

Orthodox Qabalists believe that Hebrew is the most sacred of all languages, and that the letters of the Hebrew alphabet are both the building blocks of creation and the tools that put them all together. They believe the Holy Scriptures were divinely inspired and originally written in Hebrew to veil and reveal layer upon layer of ever-deepening spiritual truth. Certainly for devoted Jewish Qabalists this is the case, whether or not there is any historic validity to their belief or not.

As a Chicken Qabalist I have the greatest respect for the remarkable way parts of the Bible yield astounding treasures to the tinkering student. Furthermore, I give thanks to the Great Poulterer that

we have at our disposal that vast body of sectarian literature—
hundreds of years of self-referential material, including classic
Qabalistic texts, that employ biblical passages as springboards for the
most illuminating exegesis. This material remains the foundation of
our study whether or not we choose to embrace any of the religious
aspects of the work (and this, dear students, is what separates us from
our orthodox brothers and sisters)—we are not Qabalists to prove the
Bible is holy—we are Qabalists because *everything* is holy. *Look hard
enough at anything and you will eventually see everything!* Right now—
right where you are, God is talking to you from the pages of the
Bible, the Koran, the Vedas—from the funny papers, billboards,
street signs, ticket stubs, and automobile license plates.

We don't always have to be quick to tinker with the letters and
numbers when we use the techniques of Gematria, Notariqon, or
Temura. We are perpetually bombarded by countless numbers nestled within the billions of impressions we process each day. How
many times a day do we write the date? What is 57 doing on a jar of
pickles? We listen to the Top 40, watch the News at 7 and go to work
by taking the 405 freeway to the 55 to the 5 to the 101.

The ancient Qabalists didn't spend much time on the turnpike
and probably didn't listen to the Top 40. What they did do was spend
a lot of time studying the scriptures, and as the Tenth Command-
Rant informs us, the scriptures are certainly as holy as a jar of pickles.

As a matter of fact, the Bible is already crawling with numbers.
Perhaps you'd like a better understanding of what Ezekiel was talking
about in his famous vision? A clue might be found in the very first
chapter and verse of his book. In English it reads:

> *Now it came to pass in the thirtieth year, in the fourth month,
> in the fifth day of the month, as I was among the captives by the
> river of Chebar, that the Heavens were opened, and I saw
> visions of God.*[1]

I personally do not think it was important for Ezekiel to make sure
we all knew the exact publication date of his book. I do, however,

think that he wanted to make it perfectly clear that he might be writing about something other than his psychedelic escapades with flying saucers, four-headed aliens, and dancing skeletons.

In the first verse we find the numbers 30, 4 and 5, or the Hebrew letters ל-L, ד-D, and ה-H, or the Hebrew word לדה which means "birth."

The second verse has a similar message: *In the fifth day of the month, which was the fifth year of King Jehoiachin's captivity,* we find 5 (ה-H), and 5 (ה-H) (duh!)—or the Hebrew word הה, which means "window!" A window is something through which we observe. It also permits light to enter. *Birth, the result of penetrating light?* Light penetrating where? The Book of Ezekiel sounds a little more intriguing now doesn't it? Take a peak at how chapter 8 starts out:

> *And it came to pass in the sixth year, in the sixth month, in the fifth day of the month, as I sat in mine house, and the elders of Judah sat before me, that the hand of the Lord GOD fell there upon me.* (Ezekiel 8:1).

We find the numbers 6, 6, and 5. I couldn't find any significant words spelled VVH or even HVV, but when I put the three numbers side-by-side, I see the number 665 which is the sum of the Hebrew words בית הרחם, "the womb," which certainly seems to carry on the theme that was started in chapter 1: verse 1. *Light penetrating the womb which gives birth*—gives birth to what?

The 20th chapter may tell us. It begins with even more numbers:

> *And it came to pass in the seventh year, in the fifth month, the tenth day of the month, that certain of the elders of Israel came to inquire of the LORD, and sat before me.* (Ezekiel 20:1).

Number 7,510? Well, we can really get bogged down on numbers that large, but if we reduce the 10 to a 1 we get the number 751, which is the sum of the Hebrew word for "finished man" or "perfect man": איש תם, or AYSh ThM. Thus, by investigating the numbers that are mentioned openly in these four verses, we find ourselves teased with the concept of *Light penetrating the womb giving birth to the Perfected Man.*

Was that the message Ezekiel was trying to convey? Probably not. But who cares! Whatever it was that the old boy was originally trying to say shrinks to insignificance. It is far more important to *my* spiritual enlightenment that my mind was forced to churn at breakneck speed to put all of this together, and then open itself up to the infinite potentialities of meaning. *Look hard enough at anything and you will eventually see everything!* It doesn't even have to make very much sense what you connect to what. It's all ultimately connected! Don't you see?

The Qabalah doesn't enable me to merely interpret what somebody else meant to say; it forces me to hear what I need to hear! Each time I make another connection on paper, I am creating a new connection in my head (or perhaps reattaching a connection that was disconnected from the heads of our ancestors vast ages ago), and I am one step nearer to the realization that everything in Heaven and Earth is connected to everything in Heaven and Earth.

I'll now leave Ezekiel to the pizza cutter of your own wit. Time is short. I must push on with subjects of Gematria, Notariqon, and Temura, by which we can wring more truths (and Holy lies) from numbers and words. Please remember that these are not the only ways to warm up your cosmic translator, but they certainly are three classic, tried-and-true methods of the Chicken Qabalist.

GEMATRIA

Gematria[2] is the process by which each letter of a word or series of words is converted to its numerical equivalent. Words yielding the same value are connected by their common numerical vibration and (on one plane or another) descriptive of each other. These correspondences are seldom obvious, and it is the student's quest to meditate upon the words and numbers until he or she achieves the level of consciousness in which the illusory contradictions are resolved.

For example, The Hebrew word for "riches" and "power" is דבא (DBA). The three letters add to the sacred number 7. If we spell DBA backward, we get the word אבד (ABD) which means "loss" or "ruin."

While it doesn't take a rocket-scientist to realize that the opposite of "riches" and "power" is "loss" and "ruin," the order and meanings of the individual Hebrew letters in these words tell a simple but profound story.

The Hebrew word "riches" דבא (DBA) suggests a *door* ד to a *house* ב or *barn* opening to enclose an *ox* א (an ancient symbol of wealth).

However, the word for "loss" or "ruined" reverses the letters and suggests the *ox* א of wealth finds the *barn's door* ב ד and escapes. Or, to put it bluntly: Door + Barn + Ox = Good! Ox + Barn + Door = Bad!

Another famous paradox of Gematria demonstrates that the Hebrew word for Messiah משיח (MShYCh) and the word used to describe the serpent נחש (NChSh) that tempted Eve in the Garden of Eden both add to 358. Could this mean that the serpent might be the savior of the world, and the Messiah might lead us to damnation?

Christians certainly think "Jesus" (יהושוה = 326) is the "Lord" (בל = 32), and those two words together = 358 = Messiah. I bet they'd be surprised, however, to learn that every time they dutifully end their prayers in the "name" (שם = 340) "Jesus" (יהושוה = 326), they are Qabalistically invoking 666, the number of the Beast of the *Book of the Revelation,* and for many, one of the scariest anti-Christian characters in the Bible. Could it be we really don't understand the meaning of either of these concepts and the number 358 might be our only clue?

Now, I'm sure you're asking yourselves, "How did Rabbi Ben Clifford know that all these Hebrew words added to these numbers?" Well, you may not believe this but, in 1979, I took a few months off and rented a cabin in upstate New York, where I added up every Hebrew word in the Bible, a well as in all the major Qabalistic texts, and put them in my Rolodex. It's so big I have to keep it in the garage because my Mom says it's a breeding-ground for dust mites.[3]

Table 4 is a quick and dirty view of English letters, their Hebrew counterparts and numerical equivalents.[4]

Table 4. English Alphabet with Possible Hebrew Numerations.

Letter	Number	Letter	Number
A	1 or 70	N	50 (also 700 as a Final N)
B	2		
C	20 or 100 (if hard like "cake") 60 (if soft like "cider")	O	70 or 6
		P	80 (also 800 as a Final P)
Ch	8 (as in "chief" or "chug." Ch can also be pronounced the same as H)	Q	100 or 20
		R	200
		S	60
D	4	Sh	300
E	5	T	9
F	6 or 80	Th	400
G	3	Tz	90 (also 900 as a Final Tz)
H	5		
I	10	U	6
J	10	V	6
		W	6
K	20 (also 500 as a Final K) or 100	X	90 or 8
L	30	Y	10
M	40 (also 600 as a Final M)	Z	7

Some letters have multiple numbers because phonetically they can sound like other letters and those other letters have different numbers. For example, the English word "cat" could be spelled many ways using Hebrew letters. Just a few ways it could be spelled are shown below:

חאט (ChAT = 18)   חאת (ChATh = 409)

כאט (KAT = 30)   קאט (QAT = 110)

כאת (KATh = 421)   קאת (QATh = 501)

As Hebrew doesn't use any vowels, "cat" can also be spelled with just the consonants:

חט (ChT = 17)   חת (ChTh = 408)

כט (KT = 29)   כת (KTh = 420)

קט (QT = 109)   קת (QTh = 500)

The numeration of the word changes, with variations in spelling offering us more food for thought and more opportunity for intellectual overload so coveted by Chicken Qabalists. As far as I'm concerned, all spelling is equally correct as long as it evokes a chain reaction of thoughts. The Chicken Qabalist should feel free to transliterate English letters and words using a broad assortment of methods. For example, if I change each English letter of my name to a logical Hebrew counterpart (a very un-Hebrew thing to do) we arrive at the number 419:

LAMED
30 + 1 + 40 + 5 + 4   = 80
BEN
2 + 5 + 50   = 57
CLIFFORD
20 + 30 + 10 + 6 + 6 + 6 + 200 + 4   = 282
                                       = **419**

Now 419 is a very interesting number. First of all, it is a Prime Number and cannot be divided by any other number but itself. There are some pretty important Hebrew words that add to 419. The word for the Hebrew letter Teth (טית) adds to 419. טית means "serpent" and all the wonderful and scary things that go with the idea of serpent. According to our Sepher Yetzirah, Teth is the letter of the zodiac sign of Leo. On the Tree of Life, Teth is the path that joins the fourth Sephirah, Chesed, to the fifth Sephirah, Geburah. In the Tarot, Teth is the *Strength* card.

Wow! Isn't 419 a great number? But if we look a little deeper, we discover that the Hebrew words Sodom and Gomorah (סדם עמרה) also add to 419, and we know what the Bible tells us happened to those communities. Oops! Maybe I better spell my name differently. In more strict Hebrew, it might be spelled as follows:

LMD		
30 + 40 + 4	= 74	
BN		
2 + 50	= 52	
CLPhRD		
20 + 30 + 80 + 200 + 4	= 334	
	= 460	

But 460 is also a wonderful number (and a big number in traditional Judaism) because it is the sum of the letters of the words "Holiness to the Lord" (קדש ליהוה). These words were engraved upon a gold plate that the High Priest of Israel wore on his hat.

My first name can further be reduced to the simple letter L (ל), which, after all, is spelled LMD למד and rendered "Lamed" in English. I can also treat the "C" in Clifford as a "Q," and we get the following:

L		
30	= 30	
BN		
2 + 50	= 52	
QLPhRD		
100 + 30 + 80 + 200 + 4	= 414	
	= 496	

Here a very interesting number. Hebrew words that add to 496 include the great sea-devil Leviathan (לויתן) and Malkuth (מלכות), the tenth and lowest Sephirah on the Tree of Life.

Determining a word's number is only the beginning of the fun. Next we pick the number apart by every means known and a few that we will make up. For example: 496 is the sum of the numbers 1 through 31. (In other words, if 496 was a barrel of wine, 31 would be the brandy distilled from that wine.) Turning to one of our number texts[5] we find that 31 has several entries. The two most important, in my opinion, are AL (אל) which is the simplest way to say God in Hebrew, and LA (לא) which means "not." This reminds us of the first two Command-Rants; All is One, AL (אל) and All is Nothing, LA (לא). Say what you will about Islam, but Allah is a great name for God!

There are no hard and fast rules about how you go about chasing one number to another. Go crazy. That's the idea![6] Feel free to break into other levels of correspondences. For instance: 496 = Malkuth, and on the Tree of Life it is 10, and represents the material plane. That means that 496 must also represent all things 10ish (after all 4 + 9 + 6 = 19 and 1 + 9 = 10). The Hebrew letter Yod enumerates to 10. Yod means "hand." Using Hebrew for English, HA (הא) means "this" and ND (נד) means "a skin bottle." Also, HAND (האנד) = 60. The number 60 is the Hebrew letter ס (Samekh) which suggests the phallus (Oh my God! *This skin bottle!*) and when spelled in full is סמך SMK, which enumerates to 120, which is the number of the word "on," the sacred Greek word for "existence" and "being,"[7] and one of the most holy Egyptian words for Deity in the person of the Sun.

See what we've done? Even this little excursion around Gematrialand has rewarded us with the provocative revelation that Yod, the creative hand of God, and the essence of existence and being, manifests as the Sun in our *macro*cosmic solar system, and also as the human phallus (*this skin bottle, no less!*) in the *micro*cosmic material plane of Malkuth, the 10th and lowest Sephirah on the Tree of Life—whose number is 496.

What does this all mean? Who cares!

You can see where this is all going, can't you? Like a mountain goat leaping ecstatically from crag to crag, one thought springs into another, and another, ad infinitum. You can continue, almost forever, connecting things that you never thought were connected. Sooner or later something's going to snap and you will overcome the *fundamental defect in your powers of perception.*

But don't expect illumination to come as the result of some particular revelation concerning numbers or language. No, no, no, my children! Getting all worked up over those discoveries will chase away your friends and ruin your social life. Your Qabalistic enlightenment will come quietly from the simple, but profound, realization that you are integrally connected to everything—just like these numbers and letters.

Now let's move on to the techniques of Notariqon and Temura. They are really elaborations on Gematria because, in the final analysis, the number of the letter or word remains of primary importance. Let's look first at Notariqon.

NOTARIQON

There are two kinds of Notariqon.[8] The first condenses a word, sentence, or a phrase into a more simple form in order to extract a more fundamental truth. The second method expands a word into a sentence whose component words are the initials of the original word.

The former is the most commonly used, and is exercised by using only the initials of the composite words to arrive at another word or number of significance. There are thousands of examples of this to be found in the Hebrew words and phrases in the Bible. Quite frankly, it's not really very impressive, because anybody can make most anything say most anything else. It all depends upon your personal or sectarian prejudices.[9] The spiritual pay-off does not come from proving a word is the perfect cryptographic definition of something else, but by breaking free of our day-to-day thought patterns and realizing that anything is potentially anything else.

For our example, observe that the phrase, "I did it on time," reduces to the word "IDIOT." IDIOT = I (10) + D (4) +I (10) + O (6) + Th (400) = 430 = Nephesh, the Animal Soul of Man. (Oh God! This is getting too easy!)

The next form of Notariqon is a process that expands a letter, a word, or a sentence. For our example, let's continue the chain of ideas we started earlier and expand upon the letter Yod: Yod means "hand" and the word HAND can be expanded to reveal America's most worn out and meaningless blessing, "HAVE A NICE DAY."

But let's not stop here. When we expand "Have a nice day," we discover that the individual letters of that nauseating mantra of insincerity expand into the delicious axiom of decadence: "HEROIN AND VODKA EASE AGONY. NOTHING IS CERTAIN EXCEPT DEATH AND YESTERDAY."

What does it all mean? Who cares!

TEMURA

With Temura,[10] letters are replaced by other letters. It is the classic "secret code." There are infinite ways this can be done, so I will only show you a few. The most primitive form of Temura simply rearranges the letters in a word or phrase. Let's look at the phrase "HAVE A NICE DAY." It can be rearranged to yield all sorts of profundities.

◆ You may start your day with the simple affirmation— EACH DAY NAÏVE

◆ Or coldly curse people by telling them to "HAVE AN ICE DAY."

◆ You might suggest a dessert to your friend, "HAVE A ICE, ANDY."

◆ Or meet someone at the uncomfortable corner of HAY AND ICE AVE.

◆ Did you ever begin your prayer to David, the patron saint of outlaw motorcyclists?—AVE, CHAIN DAVE.

◆ Movie villains may ask, "CAN A HEAVY DIE?"

◆ What a stupid question. Of course, A HEAVY CAN DIE.

◆ You might admire someone's firm handshake and exclaim, "YEA! A VICE HAND."

◆ You might eat too much chocolate and have to warn people, "I HEAVE A CANDY!"

◆ Your dentist might make you wear a sign that says I A DECAY HAVEN.

◆ Or she may cruelly admonish you, HA! NAÏVE DECAY!

◆ To honor dead spies, paradise might host a yearly CIA HEAVEN DAY.

◆ A hypochondriac might try to color his imaginary illness and DYE A VAIN ACHE.

Unfortunately, none of the above statements make any sense—but who cares! Look at all the unconnected things that got themselves connected. However, if we were dealing with Hebrew letters and words that have their own numerical equivalents and multiple definitions, we might find all sorts of entertaining and enlightening messages.

The most common way Qabalists replace one letter with another is by utilizing a table called AIQ BKR, or The Qabalah of the Nine Chambers. See Table 5, page 195.

Letters having the same single digit root [1-10-100], [2-20-200], [3-30-300], etc.) are grouped together in nine chambers. The letter A can be replaced by I (or J or Y) or Q. The letter B can be

Table 5. The Qabalah of the Nine Chambers.

A	I, J, Y	Q	B	K	R	G	L	Sh
1	10	100	2	20	200	3	30	300
D	M	Th	H	N	K	V,W	S	M
4	40	400	5	50	*Final*	U,O	60	*Final*
					500	6		600
Z	Ay, O	N	Ch	P	P	T	Tz	Tz
7	70	*Final*	8	80	*Final*	9	90	*Final*
		700			800			900

replaced by K or R, thus the name AIQ BKR. The Hebrew word for "bull," PR פר (280) could be replaced by the Hebrew word for "bosom" ChB חב (10). The English word LID (34) conceals the word ShAM (341).

The Qabalah of the Nine Chambers (Table 5) is particularly helpful for those Chicken Qabalists who dabble with Magick Squares. A Magick Square is really the numerical matrix of its parent Sephirah on the Tree of Life. In other words, Binah is the third Sephirah, and therefore is the Sephiratic expression of the planet Saturn. Consequently, the Magick Square of Saturn is a square 3 x 3.

This follows right down the Tree of Life and right up the number scale: the Magick Square of Jupiter (4th Sephirah, Chesed) is a square 4 x 4; the Magick Square of Mars (5th Sephirah, Geburah) is a square 5 x 5; the Magick Square of the Sun (6th Sephirah, Tiphareth) is a square 6 x 6; the Magick Square of Venus (7th Sephirah, Netzach) is a square 7 x 7; the Magick Square of Mercury (8th Sephirah, Hod) is a square 8 x 8; and the Magick Square of Luna (9th Sephirah, Yesod) is a square 9 x 9.

These Magic Squares (see figure 39, page 196) are filled with numbers—the same amount of numbers as there are squares in the Magic Square. Thus, the Magick Square of Saturn/Binah (3 x 3 = 9)

Saturn

4	9	2
3	5	7
8	1	6

Jupiter

4	14	15	1
9	7	6	12
5	11	10	8
16	2	3	13

Mars

11	24	7	20	3
4	12	25	8	16
17	5	13	21	9
10	18	1	14	22
23	6	19	2	15

Sol

6	32	3	34	35	1
7	11	27	28	8	30
19	14	16	15	23	24
18	20	22	21	17	13
25	29	10	9	26	12
36	5	33	3	2	31

Venus

22	47	16	41	10	35	4
5	23	48	17	42	11	29
30	6	24	49	18	36	12
13	31	7	25	43	19	37
38	14	32	1	26	44	20
21	39	8	33	2	27	45
46	15	40	9	34	3	28

Mercury

8	58	59	5	4	62	63	1
49	15	14	52	53	11	10	56
41	23	22	44	45	19	18	48
32	34	35	29	28	38	39	25
40	26	27	37	36	30	31	33
17	47	46	20	21	43	42	24
9	55	54	12	13	51	50	16
64	2	3	61	60	6	7	57

Luna

37	78	29	70	21	62	13	54	5
6	38	79	30	71	22	63	14	46
47	7	39	80	31	72	23	55	15
16	48	8	40	81	32	64	24	56
57	17	49	9	41	73	33	65	25
26	58	18	50	1	42	74	34	66
67	27	59	10	51	2	43	75	35
36	68	19	60	11	52	3	44	76
77	28	69	20	61	12	53	4	45

Figure 39. Planetary Magick Squares.

will contain the numbers 1–9; the Square of Jupiter/Chesed 1–16; the Square of Mars/Geburah 1–25; the Square of Sol/Tiphareth 1–36; the Square of Venus 1–49; the Square of Mercury 1–64; and the Square of Luna 1–81.

The numbers of all Magick Squares are ingeniously arranged such that the sum of the integer in any horizontal, vertical, or main diagonal line is always the same.

You will also notice that the numbers 1 through 10 and the numbers 20, 30, 40, 50, 60, 70, and 80 are in bold type wherever they appear in the various Magick Squares. This is because these numbers also represent Hebrew letters. Qabalistic magicians have for centuries used these Magick Squares to create the sigils or signatures of angels and various other spiritual beings who personify various aspects of each individual Sephirah. These sigils capture the mathematical essence of the spirit. They can be used to charge talismans or amulets, or when drawn in the air with a magic wand, evoke and focus the spirit's energy.

Obviously all the Hebrew letters cannot be represented by all the squares. Even the biggest square, that of Luna, has only 81 squares, completely leaving out room for the letters, Tzaddi (90), Qoph (100), Resh (200), Shin (300), and Tav (400).

The poor Magick Square for Saturn has only 9 numbers/letters to work with. How could I create the sigil for the bumbling nerd Angel named DORKAEL[11] on the Saturn Magick Square? (See figure 40 below.) I can find the 4 for D and the 6 for O and the 1 for A and the 5 for E, but what do I do for the R and the K and the L? 200 and 20 and 30 don't appear on the Magick Square of Saturn. Am I out of luck? No!

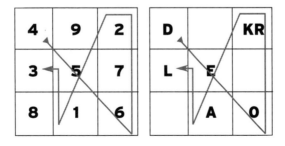

Figure 40. Creating a Sigil.

K	I	T	Ch	Z	V	H	D	G	B	A
L	M	N	S	O	P	Tz	Q	R	Sh	Th

Figure 41. The AthBSh.

K	I	T	Ch	Z	V	H	D	G	B	A
M	N	S	O	P	Tz	Q	R	Sh	Th	L

Figure 42. The ALBth.

That's where the Qabalah of the Nine Chambers (Table 5) comes in. I look up R in the Nine Chambers' chart and see that R (200) shares its chamber with K (20) and B (2). There isn't a 20 in the Magick Square of Saturn but there is a 2. So, in creating the sigil for DORKAEL, I will treat the 200 of R as the 2 of B and use the square of 2. I will also have to use the 2 square for the K as well.

Other techniques of Temura divide the alphabet in two parts in various ways and replace letters with the letter in the box above or below it. The version in figure 41 (above) is called AThBSh (after the first four letters in the code).

The version of Temura in figure 42 is called ALBTh (after the first four letters in its code).

As you can imagine, there are nearly infinite ways to rearrange the letters so that they . . . [12]

    . . . rearranging the letters . . . to peel back . . .
        . . . infinite ways . . .
            . . . all we can do is rearrange . . .
    . . . it just looks like creation . . .

Sometimes it is so . . . . We don't really climb the Tree of Life to get back to the Godhead . . . we just peel back . . . peel back . . . like Solomon in the nut garden[13] . . . one membrane peeled back to reveal another and another . . . the center germ of the nut is invisible . . . is nothing . . . yet it carries the code of all of its ancestors and the potential of infinite nuts to come . . . I'm that center germ . . . not the shell, not the meat, not the membranes . . . .I'm the nothing in the middle.

    . . . sometimes it just becomes so very . . . .
Well, I think I've said enough about Temura and
    . . . perhaps I've just said enough now.

    Please excuse me.

    You know, dear friends, when all is said and done, it makes no difference how we rearrange or substitute our letters. It makes no difference if one number reveals another number, or word, or—or any of it—as long as all this helps us make a final connection. Because, at the end of the day, it really doesn't matter what we've done, only that we *did*.

    Every letter, every number, every word, every image, every concept, every thought and component of thought is at once the loving creator, offspring and destroyer of every other letter, every other number, every other word, every other image, every other concept, every other thought and component of thought.

    It's really quite lovely, actually—so tidy.

    Yes, so very tidy, and . . . and so very, very . . .

                        smooth.[14]

EPILOGUE

SHEM-HA-MEPHORASH

For I am divided for love's sake, for the chance of union.
This is the creation of the world, that the pain of division
is as nothing, and the joy of dissolution all.
—AIWASS

It is fitting that we end our study of the Chicken Qabalah of Rabbi Lamed Ben Clifford with what I believe to be his greatest work, *The Secret of Shem-ha-Mephorash.* This tiny masterpiece was meticulously hand-printed on the back cover of his *Games Qabalists Play* notebook, and could very well be the last words he ever wrote.

Shem-ha-Mephorash means "divided name," and has traditionally been the subject of much Qabalistic speculation and discussion. Unfortunately, with the exception of his *Secret of the Shem-ha-Mephorash*, the Rabbi has left us with no written or recorded comments on the subject.[1]

We have every reason to believe Ben Clifford wrote these words shortly after the abrupt and enigmatic conclusion of *Games Qabalists Play* and shortly before his disappearance. In my opinion, he had broken through, at least temporarily, to the level of transcendent illumination that he had worked so hard to achieve. I believe it was in the white-heat of this exaltation that he penned the last seventy-two words of Rabbi Lamed Ben Clifford.

The Secret of the Shem-Ha-Mephorash

THE LAST WRITTEN WORDS OF RABBI LAMED BEN CLIFFORD

God is.

Undivided God is pure potentiality
and realizes Nothing.

God can only realize Itself by becoming Many
and then experiencing all possibilities
through the adventures of Its many parts.

The ultimate purpose for My existence is to
exhaust My individual potentiality.

My Love for God and God's Love for Me springs from
the Great Secret we share.

The Secret is

God and I will achieve Supreme Enlightenment
at the same moment.

NOTES

FOREWORD

[1] Although I am not prepared to level any accusations at this time, it is interesting to note that the publication of DuQuette's very popular books on the occult bear an uncanny resemblance to the style and content of Rabbi Ben Clifford's unpublished writings. I will say no more.

[2] "Thelema," Greek for "will" qabalistically enumerates to the number 93.

INTRODUCTION

[1] I use the term "orthodox" in its most generic application, "conforming to established doctrines," and not in reference to specific movements within world Judaism, i.e., Orthodox vs. Reform vs. Conservative, etc.

[2] In Hebrew the root letters of the word Qabalah are Qoph ק (Q), Beth ב (B), and Lamed ל (L). For reasons which I do not altogether understand, many Jewish proponents prefer to treat the Q as a K and double the B when rendering the word into English letters.

[3] Christian students prefer to spell it *Cabala*.

[4] Ceremonial magicians prefer to spell it *Qabalah*.

[5] Gershom G. Scholem, *Zohar: The Book of Splendor: Basic Readings from the Kabbalah* (New York: Schocken Books, 1972), pp. 17 and 18.

[6] Zohar, a mystical novel based on the Torah and arguably the most famous of Qabalistic texts.

CHAPTER 0

[1] See chapter 6.

CHAPTER 1

[1] See chapter 4.

[2] See chapter 4.

[3] The Rabbi's dogmatic attitude concerning the pronunciation of Hebrew words made him the target of ridicule from nearly all quarters of the Qabalistic community. Depending upon the dialect, there are, of course, many correct ways to pronounce Hebrew words. However, the point I believe Ben Clifford was trying to make is that, so far as the study of Qabalah is concerned, pronunciation is ultimately irrelevant. Arguing over it is a waste of precious time. By assuming this cavalier attitude, the Chicken Qabalist enjoys an exhilarating level of spiritual freedom to pursue the more important aspects of the work.

[4] See chapter 2.

CHAPTER 2

[1] See chapter 3.

[2] See chapter 3.

[3] It is a Qabalistic mystery of the highest order that the three letters, AIN (meaning "not" or "Negative Existence") when reordered ANI become the Hebrew word for "I" and "Myself."

[4] Ben Clifford's translation of the Sepher Yetzirah (see chapter 3) says: "Deity . . . created the Universe (with the help of three imaginary friends, "Numbers, Letters, and Words") in 32 mysterious paths of wisdom. They consist of 10 Sephiroth out of nothing and of 22 Letters."

[5] At least *I* am real. To tell you the truth, I'm not sure about you.

[6] Isn't this a recipe for madness?—Wake up! You're already crazy— and blind, deaf, and numb to boot! See chapter 10, Gematria, Notariqon and Temura—Games Qabalists Play.

CHAPTER 3

1 Even the most respected translators of the Sepher Yetzirah admit that the source texts from which they worked contain internal inconsistencies and other obvious evidences of severe corruption. Hermetic Qabalists of the 19th and 20th centuries (particularly the adepts of the Golden Dawn) freely adjusted certain planetary and zodiacal letter assignments to conform to modern and universally acknowledged astrological standards. Rabbi Ben Clifford's "translation" conforms to this modern tradition.

2 See chapter 7.

3 The Biblical translations here are obviously those of the Rabbi himself, who worked from the standard Hebrew texts.

4 Editor's note: Ben Clifford claimed that when he was born, his mother, who at the time was a groupie with the Cliffy Eban Klezmer Band, was unsure exactly who fathered her child. She wished to name him "El" after God, but her colleagues cautioned her that to do so might be considered a blaspheme. Instead, she named him simply "L," which in English is pronounced "El" and is rendered ל, Lamed, in Hebrew.

5 It might surprise you to know that traditionally the concept of God as a father is foreign to the ancient Jewish mind. Abraham was the father of the Jews, and the father figure *to* the Jews. In the Bible, Abraham never referred to God as father, neither did Noah, Moses, Elijah, Elias, Jeremiah, Ezekiel, Amos, Jonah, Solomon, Ezra, or Nehemiah. In fact, in the entire Old Testament only two verses in the book of Isaiah and one Psalm of David make reference to the father-like qualities of Deity.

6 Qabalists are quick to point out that because the phrase אלהים ויאמר, "and God said" (literally "and said Elohim") appears ten times in the first chapter of Genesis, that the number 10 is the key number of creation.

7 The Gospel According to Saint John, 1:1.

8 The element Earth, like Malkuth, the lowest Sephiroth, is some-

what of a cosmic stepchild. It is represented by a Hebrew letter (ת, Tau), which also represents the planet Saturn. Early in the creation scenario, however, the three primitive and primary elements were Air, Water, and Fire.

9 Some Hebrew letters look very much like other letters. We will learn more about this in chapter 4.

CHAPTER 4

1 Some of you may already have a good working knowledge of the Hebrew alphabet, and will be tempted to skip over the next section. Please resist such temptation, and read it through at least once. You may learn a thing or two you don't already know. At the very least, it may help you with your Hebrew penmanship.

CHAPTER 5

1 Pronounce it any way you want.

2 Peh פ, can also be pronounced like an "F." פ פ could also be pronounced "faf," or "fafe," or "feef," or "fif," or "fife," or "fof," or "fofe," or "fuf," or "fafa," or "faffy," or "fofeye," or "feefee," or "foofoo."

3 Editor's note: Here again, the Rabbi's penchant for the dramatic becomes evident. It is clear that the High Priest did not always die in a spectacular explosion. It is most likely, however, that it was expected that he would be rendered unconscious by the act of touching the Ark and uttering the Ineffable Name.

4 Editor's note: Rabbi Ben Clifford is quite correct concerning the use of battle gods by ancient peoples. However, his reference here to monumental talismanic totem cheeses appears to be completely devoid of historic or traditional foundation.

5 Editor's note: Aaron's rod was a staff of almond wood that, at a very auspicious moment, miraculously bloomed. The Hebrew words for "a rod of almond" (מטה השקד) enumerate to the prime number 463. The three Hebrew letters that enumerate to 463 are ת, ס, and ג (Tau, Samekh, and Gimel). On the Tree of Life (see page 43) Tau,

Samekh, and Gimel form the middle pillar—the most balanced and direct path from material existence to supreme godhead—of which the human spine is the microcosmic reflection. Whatever material Aaron's rod was actually made of, it was described as being "a rod of almond" in order to communicate to anyone interested in how it worked. It is not unreasonable to speculate that a central rod (middle pillar) running between a positive current (the right-hand Pillar of Severity) and a negative current (the left-hand Pillar of Mildness) might be an object containing magnetic or electrical properties.

6 About 3 ¾ feet (about 1.1 meters) long and 2 ¼ feet (about 0.7 meter) wide and high.

7 Also called an atonement cover.

8 About 3 ¾ feet (about 1.1 meters) long and 2 ¼ feet (about 0.7 meter) wide.

9 "Then Solomon assembled all the tribes of Israel, all the heads of the tribes, and the chiefs of the fathers, to him in Jerusalem to bring up the ark of the covenant of יהוה out of the city of David which is Zion . . . . And the priest brought in the ark of the covenant of יהוה to its place, into the temple, to the inner house, the Holy of Holies, under the wings of the cherubim . . . . And when the priests came out of the holy place, a cloud filled the house of יהוה so that the priests could not stand to minister because of the cloud; for the glory of יהוה had filled the house of יהוה (1 Kings 8:1, 6, 10–11).

10 Editor's note: Ben Clifford is correct. Crude batteries, metal-lined pots containing what appears to be a solution of crushed grapes and rods, have been found in Egyptian tombs. There is speculation that such devices helped provide light to the workers and artisans in their subterranean workplace.

CHAPTER 6

1 "Once Hollywood sees my idea on paper, they will immediately recognize it as boffo and give me lots of money to produce it. "

2 Pronounce *it* any way you want.

CHAPTER 7

1 It was first published in 1652, in Athanasius Kircher's *Oedipus Ægyptiacus*.

2 Sephirah is the singular form.

3 See chapter 3.

4 Editor's note. There is no chapter eleven in the book of Ezra.

5 For the moment, the Rabbi's fantasy is forgetting the books of the Prophets which are also sources of rich Qabalistic speculation.

6 There certainly *is* no ambiguity about the documents. They were fabricated entirely by Rabbi Ben Clifford and written with a No. 2 graphite pencil on sheets of modern history notebook paper.

7 There is perhaps no more pathetic example of Rabbi Ben Clifford's naivete than his inclusion of the B.C. designation date upon a supposedly authentic ancient document.

8 See chapter 6.

9 Atziluth, the Archetypal World; Briah, the Creative World; Yetzirah, the Formative World ; and Assiah, the Material World. See chapter 6.

10 Chiah, the Life-Force; Neshamah, the Divine Soul Intuition; Ruach, the Intellect; and Nephesh, the Animal Soul. See chapter 6.

11 See chapter 6.

CHAPTER 8

1 *The Book of the Goetia of Solomon the King. Translated into the English Tongue by a Dead Hand and adorned with Divers Other Matter Germane Delightful to the Wise, the Whole Edited, Verified, Introduced and Commented by Aleister Crowley.* The most recent edition contains engraved illustrations of the spirits by M. L. Breton and a foreword by Hymenaeus Beta (York Beach, ME: Samuel Weiser, 1996). It is known as *The Lesser Key of Solomon*, the First Book of the Lemegeton (c. 1687), translated by S. L. MacGregor Mathers (the "Dead Hand" referred to in the full title above), from the British Library Sloane Manuscripts nos. 2731 and 3648.

2 Spirit of Venus.

3 There is no argument that individuals who have a general understanding of nutrition and anatomy have a better chance of staying healthy than those who do not. For most of us, however, it is not necessary to memorize the name of every bone and muscle in order to stay healthy.

CHAPTER 9

1 *Sic*. The word Qabalah was misspelled throughout the interview. For my own sanity I have corrected it in the rest of the interview.—Ed.
2 Hermit = ' = "I," Magician = ב = "B," Hanged Man = מ = "M."
3 It is always wise to check the Sun degrees out with an ephemeris to get the most accurate dates in any given year.

CHAPTER 10

1 *The Holy Bible*, George M. Lamsa, trans. (Philadelphia: A. J Holman Company, 1967).
2 Pronounce it any way you want.
3 This statement is a complete and utter lie! It is without a doubt the most blatant falsehood Ben Clifford ever offered. According to his closest disciples, no such Rolodex ever existed. The Rabbi used a variety of lexicons and texts that were readily available at the time. In fact, Ben Clifford was often seen clutching his tattered copy of *777*, the Qabalah of Aleister Crowley (*777 and Other Qabalistic Writings*, published by Samuel Weiser in 1970, 1981, 1986, and still today) that contains Sepher Sephiroth, a compilation of significant Hebrew words and their numerical equivalents.
4 For a more complete chart, see chapter 4.
5 Aleister Crowley, *777 and Other Qabalistic Writings*, Israel Regardie, ed.
6 Editor's note: What follows is a classic example of Ben Clifford's slide into the disciplined "madness" symptomatic of the early stages of Qabalistic illumination. Please make every attempt to follow the process. When the chain of his ill-logic begins to actually make sense

to you, you are "on your way" to Qabalistic illumination. (Caution: when this occurs, it is likely that you will become giddy with Qabalistic fervor. At such a time, it is unwise to try to share your illumination with family and friends. You might find yourself "on your way" to the rubber room hotel.)

[7] As in "ontology," the metaphysical study of the nature of being or reality.

[8] Pronounce it any way you want.

[9] Editor's note: I cannot resist reprinting the following excerpt from my book, *Angels, Demons & Gods of the New Millennium* (York Beach, ME: Samuel Weiser, 1997), p. 30. I think the Rabbi would have been amused:

> Perhaps the most famous example [of Notariqon] is BRAShITh, the first word of Genesis commonly translated "In the beginning." B-R-A-Sh-I-Th can be expanded to say—BRAShITh RAH ALHIM ShIQBLV IShRAL ThVRH: "In the beginning Elohim saw that Israel would accept the law." The shortcomings of this exercise are obvious, for while the above sentence may have profound meaning to a Qabalist who is an orthodox Jew, the Christian Qabalist might prefer Prosper Rugere's interpretation— BBVA RBN AShR ShMV IShVo ThOBVDV: "When the Master shall come Whose name is Jesus ye shall worship." Then again, the diabolist might argue that B-R-A-Sh-I-Th really means—BRAShITh RAH AShMDAI ShIQBLV IShRAL ThChLVM: "In the beginning Asmodai (the demon king) saw that Israel would accept hallucinations."

[10] Pronounce it any way you want.

[11] Ben Clifford appears to have invented an angel just for the purpose of illustration.

[12] It is at this point that Ben Clifford's last essay begins to quickly disintegrate. I've attempted to replicate the broken word placement of the original handwritten manuscript. I believe it allows us a rare and poignant glimpse of the moment when his Ruach finally loosened its

iron grip on his self-identity, allowing him to more perfectly identify with the higher aspects of his soul.

13 Song of Songs, 6:11.

14 The Smooth Point. One of the traditional titles of Kether.

EPILOGUE

1 For the benefit of readers who are not familiar with the basic traditional concepts behind the *Shem-ha-Mephorash,* I have included in the glossary a portion of my book, *Angels, Demons & Gods of the New Millennium,* which discusses in detail this fascinating aspect of the Qabalah.

GLOSSARY

1 York Beach, ME: Samuel Weiser, 1997, p. 39.

2 English translation from *The Holy Bible from Ancient Eastern Manuscripts,* George M. Lamsa, trans. (Philadelphia: A. J. Holman Company, 1967), Exodus 14:19–21.

GLOSSARY

AIN—Nothing: Profound Negativity, precluding even the concept of negative existence. First of the Three Negative Veils from which Kether (One) emerges.

AIN-SOPH—Nothing Without Limit: Second of the Three Negative Veils from which Kether (One) emerges.

AIN-SOPH-AUR—Limitless Light: Third and last of the Three Negative Veils from which Kether (One) emerges.

AIQ BKR—The Qabalah of the Nine Chambers: A nine-chambered cryptographic table in which the 22 Hebrew letters and their finals are arranged according to their decimal similarities. [1-10-100, 2-20-200, 3-30-300, 4-40-400, 5-50-500, 6-60-600, 7-70-700, 8-80-800, 9-90-900]. *See* **Temura.**

ATZILUTH—The Archetypal World: The fourth and highest of the four Qabalistic Worlds; corresponds to the Yod in the Tetragrammaton; the element Fire; and the suit of Wands in the tarot. In Atziluth the male and female aspects of the Deity are united in bliss. The remaining three worlds (Briah, Yetzirah, and Assiah) are the product of this union, and continue to diminish in purity. Atziluth could be considered the Will of the Deity in its purest aspect. The Atziluth's corresponding part in the human soul is the Chiah—the Life-Force.

ASSIAH—The Material World: The first and lowest of the four Qabalistic Worlds; corresponds to the final Heh of the Tetragrammaton; the element Earth; and the suit of Disks in the tarot. In Assiah the impurities produced by the degeneration of the light as it passes through the worlds above it (Atziluth, Briah, and Yetzirah) are crystallized to form the Material World, and human existence. Assiah's corresponding part in the human Soul is the Nephesh—the Animal Soul.

BINAH—Understanding: The Third Sephirah of the Tree Life; Shabbathai—The Sphere of Saturn; *Divine Name (in Atziluth):* YHVH Elohim (Lord God); *Archangel (in Briah):* Tzaphqiel (Who covers God); *Angelic Choir (in Yetzirah):* The Aralim (Mighty Ones); *Angel (in Yetzirah)*: Cassiel; *Intelligence (in Assiah)*: Agiel; *Spirit (in Assiah)*: Zazel.

BRIAH—The Creative World: The third and second highest of the four Qabalistic Worlds; corresponds to the first Heh of the Tetragrammaton; the element Water; and the suit of Cups in the tarot. In Briah the pure light of Atziluth begins to become organized. This is the throne and abode of the highest Archangels and could be viewed as the Heart of the Deity. Briah's corresponding part in the human soul is the Neshamah—the Divine Soul Intuition.

CHESED—Mercy: The Fourth Sephirah of the Tree Life; Tzedek—The Sphere of Jupiter. *Divine Name (in Atziluth):* El; *Archangel (in Briah):* Tzadqiel (Justice of God); *Angelic Choir (in Yetzirah):* the Cashmalim (Brilliant Ones); *Angel (in Yetzirah):* Sachiel; *Intelligence (in Assiah):* Iophiel; *Spirit (in Assiah):* Hismael.

CHIAH—The Life-Force: The fourth and highest of the four parts of the Soul; corresponds to the Yod of the Tetragrammaton, the element Fire; the suit of Wands in the tarot, and to Atziluth, the Archetypal World.

CHICKEN QABALAH: The deceptively self-effacing term given to those aspects of the Holy Hebrew Qabalah that are of *practical* value to practitioners of Western Hermetic spiritual traditions, including astrology, numerology, tarot, and several varieties of ceremonial magick.

CHOKMAH—Wisdom: The Second Sephirah of the Tree of Life; Mazloth—The Sphere of the zodiac; *Divine Name (in Atziluth):* Yah (God); *Archangel (in Briah):* Raziel (Secret of God); *Angelic Choir (in Yetzirah):* Ophanim (Wheels).

DAATH—Knowledge: A phantom, or false Sephirah, of the Tree of Life, positioned in the Abyss separating the Supernal Triad from the rest of the Tree. While knowledge is a vital and necessary tool in one's initiatory journey, the reasoning faculties have their limits, and must eventually be overcome before the highest levels of consciousness can be achieved. Daath is the false Crown of Reason, and the Abyss is the abode of Choronzon, archdemon of dispersion. It is this great devil's duty to engage the initiate in conversation—endless loops of rationalizations that prevent him or her from finally surrendering to Transcendent Consciousness.

ETZ HA-CHAYIM: *See* **Tree of Life**

GEBURAH—Strength: The Fifth Sephirah of the Tree Life; Madim—The Sphere of Mars; *Divine Name (in Atziluth):* Elohim Gibor (Almighty God); *Archangel (in Briah):* Kamael (Who sees God); *Angelic Choir (in Yetzirah):* The Seraphim (Flaming Serpents); *Angel (in Yetzirah)*: Zamael; *Intelligence (in Assiah)*: Graphiel; *Spirit (in Assiah)*: Bartzabel.

GEMATRIA: The process by which each letter of a word, or words, is converted to its numerical equivalent. Words yielding the same value are connected by their common numerical vibration and (on one plane or another) descriptive of each other.

HOD—Splendor: The Eighth Sephirah of the Tree Life; Kokab—

The Sphere of Mercury; *Divine Name (in Atziluth):* Elohim Tzabaith; *Archangel (in Briah):* Michael (Who is as God); *Angelic Choir (in Yetzirah):* The Beni Elohim (Sons of God); *Angel (in Yetzirah):* Raphael; *Intelligence (in Assiah):* Tiriel; *Spirit (in Assiah):* Taphthartharath.

KETHER—The Crown: The first and highest Sephirah of the Tree Life; Rashith ha-Gilgalim—The Sphere of the Primum Mobile; *Divine Name (in Atziluth):* Eheih (I am); *Archangel (in Briah):* Metatron (Angel of the Presence); *Angelic Choir (in Yetzirah):* Chayoth ha-Qadesh (Holy Living Creatures).

MALKUTH—Kingdom: The Tenth and lowest Sephirah of the Tree Life; the Sphere of Earth and material existence: Olam Yesodoth—The Sphere of Elements; *Divine Name (in Atziluth):* Adonai ha-Aretz (Lord of the Earth); *Archangel (in Briah):* Sandalphon (Co-brother or tall Angel); *Angelic Choir (in Yetzirah):* Eshim (Flames); *Elemental World (in Assiah):* Beneath the Angelic Choir of the Eshim, the Elemental Spirits are divided into four categories, each governed by its own individual Divine Name, Archangel, Angel, Ruler and King.

	Fire	Water	Air	Earth
Divine Name:	YHVH Tzabaoth	Elohim	Shaddai El Chai	Adonai ha-Aretz
Archangel:	Michael	Gabriel	Raphael	Auriel
Angel:	Aral	Taliahad	Chassan	Phorlakh
Ruler:	Seraph	Tharsis	Ariel	Kerub
King:	Djin	Nichsa	Paralda	Ghob

NEPHESH—The Animal Soul: The first and lowest of the four parts of the Soul; corresponds to the final Heh of the Tetragrammaton, the Earth element; the suit of Disks in the tarot, and to Assiah, the Material World, the first and lowest of the four Qabalistic Worlds.

NESHAMAH—The Soul Intuition: The third and second highest of the four parts of the Soul; corresponds to the first Heh of the Tetragrammaton, the Water element; the suit of Cups in the tarot, and to Briah, the Creative World.

NETZACH—Victory: The Seventh Sephirah of the Tree Life; Nogah—The Sphere of Venus; *Divine Name (in Atziluth):* YHVH Tzabaoth (Lord of Hosts); *Archangel (in Briah):* Haniel (Glory of God); *Angelic Choir (in Yetzirah):* The Elohim (Gods); *Angel (in Yetzirah):* Anael; *Intelligence (in Assiah):* Hagiel; *Spirit (in Assiah):* Kedemel.

NOTARIQON: There are two kinds of Notariqon. The first condenses a word, sentence, or a phrase into a more simple one by reading only the initial letters, in an attempt to retrieve a more fundamental truth. The second expands a word into a sentence whose component words are the initials of the original word.

QABALAH OF THE NINE CHAMBERS: *See* **AIK BKR.**

RUACH—The Intellect: The second of the four parts of the Soul; corresponds to the Vau of the Tetragrammaton, the Air element; the suit of Swords in the tarot, and to Yetzirah, the Formative World.

SHEM HA-MEPHORASH
The Divided Name of God. The following copy comes from my book, *Angels, Demons & Gods of the New Millennium.*[1]

One of the most impressive displays of Qabalistic gymnastics is an elaborate dissection of the Tetragrammaton called Shem-ha-Mephorash, the "divided name." Based upon the four letters of the Great Name it is one of the finest examples of how Qabalists develop new ways of viewing the dynamics of the universe and identify the spiritual agencies who run the machinery.

After exhausting all the tricks of Gematria, Notariqon, and Temura to harvest spiritual enlightenment from the Great Name, it occurred to some bright Qabalist to arrange the four letters in the form of a Pythagorean tetractys and adding the sum of the letters.

$$\text{י} = 10$$

$$\text{ה} \quad \text{י} = 15$$

$$\text{ו} \quad \text{ה} \quad \text{י} = 21$$

$$\text{ה} \quad \text{ו} \quad \text{ה} \quad \text{י} = 26$$

$$10 + 15 + 21 + 26 = 72$$

It was decided that seventy-two is a primary expression of יהוה and the key to an expanded (divided) name of God.

Now, as there are seventy-two quinaries (groups of five degrees) in the zodiac, and each of those periods of five degrees represent approximately five days of the year, it followed that each part of יהוה's divided name governed specific days of the year. This was an exciting prospect, for it promised the opportunity to more closely examine the Deity by translating the eternal and inscrutable aspects of creation into the familiar time-space language of Earth's yearly cycle. The next quest was to find the seventy-two names forming the Great Name.

Turning to the Holy Scriptures it was discovered that three consecutive verses (19, 20, 21) of chapter 14 of *Exodus* each contained exactly seventy-two letters. All that needed to be done was to Qabalistically play with these three verses until they yielded the 72 Holy Names.

It should be pointed out that these three verses are among the most significant and memorable of the entire Bible. Not only did they make Charlton Heston an immortal icon of American cinema, they narrate the story of a massive display of the Hebrew God's power manifested on Earth.

Verse 19:

וילך מאחריהם ויסע עמוד הענן מפניהם ויעמד מאחריהם:
וימע מלאך האלהים ההלך לפני מחנה ישראל

*And the angel of God, who went before the camp of Israel,
moved and went behind them; and the pillar of the cloud
moved from before them and stood behind them.*[2]

Verse 20 :

והחשך ויאר את הלילה ולא-קרב זה אל-זה כל-הלילה:
ויבא בין מחנה מצרים ובין מחנה ישראל ויהי הענן

*And it came between the army of the Egyptians and the camp
of Israel; and it was cloudy and dark all the night, but it gave
light all the night to the children of Israel, so that they could not
draw near one to another all the night.*

Verse 21:

קדים עזה כל-הלילה וישם את-הים לחרבה ו יבקעוה-מים:
ויט משה את- ידו על-הים ויולך יהוה את-הים ברוח

*And Moses lifted up his hand over the sea; and the Lord caused
the sea to go back by a strong east wind all that night and made
the sea dry land, and the waters were divided.*

They then arranged the three verses in three lines. Verse 19 on top (written from right to left); verse 20 directly beneath verse 19 (written from left to right); and verse 21 on the bottom (written from right to left). The seventy-two three-lettered names of God were then revealed in the seventy-two columns formed by this arrangement.

SUPERNAL TRIAD—Kether-Chokmah-Binah: The three Sephiroth existing above the Abyss. Even though each of the three Sephiroth stand as separate emanations, they really comprise a trinity, each reflecting a different aspect of the Supreme Monad (Kether).

TEMURA: General term for an assortment of cryptographic methods whereby one letter is substituted for another. *See* **AIQ BKR**

TIPHARETH—Beauty: The Sixth Sephirah on the Tree Life; Shemesh—The Sphere of the Sun; *Divine Name (in Atziluth):* YHVH Eloah va-Daath (Lord God of Knowledge); *Archangel (in Briah):* Raphael (God has healed); *Angelic Choir (in Yetzirah):* The Melekim (Kings); *Angel (in Yetzirah)*: Michael; *Intelligence (in Assiah)*: Nakhiel; *Spirit (in Assiah)*: Sorath.

TREE OF LIFE—Etz ha-Chayim: Schematic representation of the fundamental statement of the Sepher Yetzirah, which states (using Rabbi Ben Clifford's translation) "Deity . . . created the Universe (with the help of three imaginary friends, 'Numbers, Letters, and Words') in 32 mysterious paths of wisdom. They consist of 10 Sephiroth out of nothing and of 22 Letters." The Tree of Life is usually represented as 10 circular emanations (Sephiroth) and 22 paths to which the letters of the Hebrew alphabet are attributed.

YETZIRAH—The Formative World: The second of the four Qabalistic Worlds; corresponds to the Vau of the Tetragrammaton; the element Air; and the suit of Swords in the tarot. In Yetzirah, the universal organization of Briah becomes specific, and a hierarchy of Angels with individual duties is established. This world is the Mind and the Mind's Eye of the Deity. Yetzirah's corresponding part in the human Soul is Ruach—Intellect.

YESOD—Foundation: The Ninth Sephirah on the Tree of Life; Labanah—The Sphere of the Moon; *Divine Name (in Atziluth):* Shaddai El Chai (Almighty Living God); *Archangel (in Briah):* Gabriel (God is my strength); *Angelic Choir (in Yetzirah):* The Kerubim (who intercede); *Angel (in Yetzirah):* Also Gabriel (go figure); *Intelligence (in Assiah):* Malka be-Tarshishim ve-ad be-Ruah Shehaqim; *Spirit (in Assiah):* Chasmodai.

BIBLIOGRAPHY

Bischoff, Dr. Erich. *The Kabbala*. York Beach, ME: Samuel Weiser, 1985.

Crowley, Aleister. *The Book of Lies*. York Beach, ME: Samuel Weiser, 1992.

_____. *The Book of Thoth: A Short Essay on the Tarot of the Egyptians*. The Equinox III(5). The Master Therion. London: O.T.O., 1944. Facsimile edition, York Beach, ME: Samuel Weiser, 1974.

_____. *The Goetia: The Lesser Key of Solomon the King*. Aleister Crowley, ed. S. L. MacGregor Mathers, trans. Originally published by the Society for the Propagation of Religious Truth, in England in 1904. New edition including engraved illustrations of the spirits by M. L. Breton, and foreword by Hymenaeus Beta: York Beach, ME: Samuel Weiser, 1995.

_____. *Liber Aleph vel CXI: The Book of Wisdom or Folly*. The Equinox III(6) Rev. edition, Hymenaeus Beta, ed. York Beach, ME: Samuel Weiser, and New York: 93 Publishing, 1991.

_____. *Magick • Book Four • Liber ABA*. Hymenaeus Beta, ed. York Beach, ME: Samuel Weiser, 1993.

_____. *777 and Other Qabalistic Writings of Aleister Crowley*. Reprinted York Beach, ME: Samuel Weiser, 1990.

DuQuette, Lon Milo. *Angels, Demons & Gods of the New Millennium*. York Beach, ME: Samuel Weiser, 1997.

_____. *Tarot of Ceremonial Magick*. York Beach, ME: Samuel Weiser, 1993.

Eliade, Mircea. *A History of Religious Ideas*. London: University of Chicago Press, 1984.

Fortune, Dion. *The Mystical Qabalah.* York Beach, ME: Samuel Weiser, revised edition, 2000.

Friedman, Irving. *The Book of Creation.* New York: Samuel Weiser, 1977.

Gensenius, Wiliam. *Hebrew and Chaldee Lexicon to the Old Testament Scriptures.* S. P. Tregelles, ed. Grand Rapids, MI: Wm. Eerdmans, 1978.

James, William. *The Varieties of Religious Experience.* London: Longmans, 1910.

Jastrow, Marcus. *A Dictionary of the Targumim, the Talmud, Babi and Yerushalmi, and the Midrashic Literature.* New York: Judaica Press, 1975.

Jung, Carl G. *Man and His Symbols.* London: Aldus Books, 1964.

Kalisch, Isidor. *Sepher Yezirah: A Book on Creation, or The Jewish Metaphysics of Remote Antiquity.* New York: L. H. Frank. 1877.

Kaplan, Aryeh, ed. and trans. *The Bahir.* York Beach, ME: Samuel Weiser, 1990.

_____. ed. and trans. *Sepher Yetzerah.* York Beach, ME: Samuel Weiser, 1990.

Lamsa, George M., trans. *The Holy Bible.* Philadelphia: A. J. Holman, 1967.

Levi, Eliphas. *The Key of the Mysteries.* Aleister Crowley, trans. New York: Samuel Weiser, 1973.

Mathers, S. L. MacGregor, ed. and trans. *The Book of the Sacred Magic of Abra-Melin, the Mage.* London: Watkins, 1900; reprinted New York: Dover, 1975.

_____. ed and trans. *The Kabbalah Unveiled.* London: Kegan Paul, Trench and Trubner, 1887; reprinted York Beach, ME: Samuel Weiser, 1993.

_____. ed and trans. *The Key of Solomon the King.* London: Redway, 1889; reprinted York Beach, ME: Samuel Weiser, 1972, 1992.

Mordell, Phineas. *The Origin of Letters and Numerals According to the Sefer Yetzirah.* New York: Samuel Weiser, 1975.

Munk, Michael L. *The Wisdom in the Hebrew Alphabet.* Brooklyn: Mesorah Publications, 1983.

Ponce, Charles. *Kabbalah: An Introduction and Illumination for the World Today.* Wheaton, IL: Quest Books, 1978.

Regardie, Israel. *The Golden Dawn.* 6th edition. St. Paul: Llewellyn, 1992.

_____. *The Complete Golden Dawn System of Magic.* Phoenix, AZ: New Falcon Press, 1984.

_____. *A Garden of Pomegranates.* St. Paul: Llewellyn, 1999.

Roth, Cecil. *Encyclopedia Judaica.* New York: Macmillan, 1972.

Runyon, Carroll (Poke). *The Magick of Solomon.* Pasadena, CA: The Church of the Hermetic Sciences, 1996.

Scholem, Gershom. *Major Trends in Jewish Mysticism.* New York: Schocken Books, 1967.

_____, ed. *Zohar: The Book of Splendor: Basic Readings from the Kabbalah.* New York: Schocken Books, 1972.

Simon, M., and H. Sperling, trans. *The Zohar.* New York: Bennet, 1959.

Singer, Isidore. *The Jewish Encyclopedia.* New York: KTAV Publishing, 1964.

Sternring, Knut. *The Book of Formation.* New York: KTAV Publishing, 1970.

Suares, Carlo. *The Sepher Yetsira.* Micheline and Vincent Stuart, trans. Boulder: Shambhala, 1976.

Townley, Kevin. *The Cube of Space: Container of Creation.* Boulder: Archive Press, 1993.

Waite, Arthur Edward. *The Holy Kabbalah.* New York: University Books, 1972.

Wang, Robert. *Qabalistic Tarot.* York Beach, ME: Samuel Weiser, 1990.

Westcott, W. Wynn. *Sepher Yetzirah: The Book of Formation and the Thirty-Two Paths of Wisdom.* New York: Samuel Weiser, 1975.

INDEX

Aaron's rod, 75, 206n5
Abraham, 114
Aces, 159, 161–62, 175–76
Adam, 18, 28, 72, 125, 169
Adonai, 71
Ain, 19, 135–37, 204n3
Ain Soph, 19, 135–37
Ain Soph Aur, 19, 135–37
AIQ BKR, 194–95
Air, element, 32–33, 44, 145, 157–58, 161–62
Aiwass, 201
alchemy, 7, 150
Aleph, 32–33, 44, 55, 153
Allah, 191
Alpha and Omega, 65, 175
alphabet. *See* Hebrew alphabet
Anael, 142, 143
Angels
    example of, 140–41
    hierarchy of, 139–40, 144–45
    and Qabalistic worlds, 84–89
    and sigils, 196–97
    and spirit evocation, 130–34
    and tarot, 172
animal soul, 96–97, 103, 139, 161
Aquarius, 35, 61, 67, 154
arcana, 151–77
archangels
    example of, 140–41
    and four Qabalistic worlds, 86–89, 92, 95
    hierarchy of, 138–40, 144–45
    and spirit evocation, 130–34
Archetypal World
    hierarchy of, 139, 144–45
    and Qabalistic worlds, 90–92, 95,
        101–103
    and tarot, 160–61, 170, 174–75
Aries, 35, 42, 48, 66, 154
Ark of the Covenant, 74–77, 207n9
Assiah
    hierarchy of, 139–40, 144–45
    and Qabalistic worlds, 82–84, 92–94,
        96–97
    and tarot, 160–61, 170–73

astrology, 7, 66–67, 150, 154–56
atonement cover, 76, 207n7
Atziluth
    hierarchy of, 144–45
    and Qabalistic worlds, 90–95, 101–103,
        139–40
    and tarot, 160–61, 170, 174–75
Augury Today, journal, 1, 147–77
awareness, 99–101
Ayin, 34–35, 59

Beauty (Tipareth), 137–38, 144, 195–96
Ben Clifford, Rabbi Lamed, 1–3, 189–191,
        201–202
Ben Yehuda, Ehud, 38
Beth, 33–34, 42–43, 45
Bible
    and Chicken Qabalah, 11–12, 183–86
    and Gematria, 187, 190
    and Sepher Yetzirah, 29
    and tarot, 150
Big Bang, 101
Binah (Understanding), 136–37, 144,
        195–96
blueprint, 23–24, 84–85, 92
body, human
    and consciousness, 20
    and Nephesh, 96–97
    and Neshamah, 100–101
    and sacred numbers, 112–14, 122–23
    and Sephiroth, 30–31
    and tarot, 155–56
Book of Ezekiel, 184–86
Book of Ezra, 107–8
Book of Formation, The, 25–26, 30–36
Book of the Revelation, 187
Briah
    hierarchy of, 139–40, 144–45
    and Qabalistic worlds, 86–89, 93–95,
        99–101
    and tarot, 160–61, 170, 174

cabala. *See* Chicken Qabalah
camel, 46, 66, 153

ABOUT THE AUTHOR

L ON MILO DUQUETTE has been hailed by critics as the most entertaining author in the field of magick and the Western spiritual traditions. Often irreverently frank, his books, seminars, and workshops evoke from his audiences a curious mixture of laughter, terror, and wonderment. He is the author of numerous magical texts including *The Magick of Thelema, Tarot of Ceremonial Magick,* and *Angels, Demons, & Gods of the New Millennium*. His most recent offering is his award-winning autobiography *My Life with the Spirits,* a work which futurist and best-selling author, Robert Anton Wilson calls *". . .the best all-around introduction to Western Occultism—sane, sensible, down-to-Earth and wonderfully witty."*

Since 1975 DuQuette as been a national and international governing officer of *Ordo Templi Orientis,* one of the most influential magical societies of the 20th Century. He is a Certified Tarot Grand Master of the American Tarot Association, and prominent member of the International Tarot Society. He is married (35 years) to Constance DuQuette (his high-school sweetheart), an accomplishment he considers his greatest magical achievement.